# EYEWITNESS TRAVEL
# 15-MINUTE
# JAPANESE

D0465579

**DK** EYEWITNESS TRAVEL

# 15-MINUTE
# JAPANESE

## LEARN JAPANESE
## IN JUST 15
## MINUTES A DAY

MITSUKO MAEDA-NYE
SHIZUYO OKADA

DORLING KINDERSLEY

London, New York, Munich, Melbourne,
and Delhi

**Senior Editor** Angeles Gavira
**Senior Art Editor** Ina Stradins
**Art Editor** Hugh Schermuly
**Project Editors** Rebecca Warren,
Cathy Meeus, Shinjini Chatterjee
**Designer** Malavika Talukder
**DTP Designer** Pankaj Sharma
**Production Controller** Inderjit Bhullar
**Publishing Manager** Liz Wheeler
**Managing Art Editor** Philip Ormerod
**Publishing Director** Jonathan Metcalf
**Art Director** Bryn Walls
**Special Photographer** Mike Good

Language content for Dorling Kindersley by
g-and-w publishing

First published in Great Britain in 2006 by
Dorling Kindersley Limited
80 Strand, London WC2R 0RL
A Penguin Company
Copyright © 2006 Dorling Kindersley Limited

6 8 10 9 7

All rights reserved. No part of this publication
may be reproduced, stored in a retrieval
system, or transmitted, in any form or by
any means, electronic, mechanical,
photocopying, recording, or otherwise,
without the prior written permission
of the copyright owners.
A CIP catalogue record is available for this
book from the British Library

ISBN-13: 9781405315197

Colour reproduction by Colourscan, Singapore
Printed and bound in China by Leo Paper
Products Limited

See our complete catalogue at
www.dk.com

# Contents

営業中

# How to use this book

This main part of the book is devoted to 12 themed chapters, broken down into five 15-minute daily lessons, the last of which is a revision lesson. So, in just 12 weeks you will have completed the course. A concluding reference section contains a menu guide, an English-to-Japanese dictionary and tables of Japanese characters.

**Warm up and clock**
Each day starts with a 1-minute warm up that encourages you to recall vocabulary or phrases you have learned previously. A clock to the right of the heading bar indicates the amount of time you are expected to spend on each exercise.

**Instructions**
Each exercise is numbered and introduced by instructions that explain what to do. In some cases additional information is given about the language point being covered.

**Cultural/Conversational tip**
These panels provide additional insights into life in Japan and language usage.

**Text styles**
Japanese script and easy-to-read pronunciation are included, as well as English translation.

**In conversation**
Illustrated dialogues reflecting how vocabulary and phrases are used in everyday situations appear throughout the book.

**How to use the flap**
The book's cover flaps allow you to conceal the Japanese so that you can test whether you have remembered correctly.

**Review and repeat**
A recap of selected elements of previous lessons helps to reinforce your knowledge.

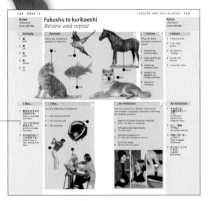

## Pronunciation guide

Most Japanese sounds will already be familiar to you, and the pronunciation guide given for all words and phrases in 15-Minute Japanese is designed to be natural to read. However, a few sounds require additional explanation:

| | |
|---|---|
| **r** | a Japanese **r** is pronounced like a cross between an English *r* and *l* |
| **ih** | *ee* as in *sheep* |
| **eh** | long *eh*, like a longer version of the sound in *they* |
| **oh** | long *o* as in *motor* |
| final **u** | the final **u** written on the end of words such as **desu** *(is/are)* and **(ga/a) arimasu** *(there is/are)* is only slightly pronounced and often sounds more like a double letter (e.g. **dess**). |

The Japanese language is based on syllables, rather than individual letters. Each syllable is pronounced with roughly equal stress.

**Useful phrases**
Selected phrases relevant to the topic help you speak and understand.

LEISURE AND SOCIALIZING **119**

**Useful phrases**

...these phrases and then test yourself using the cover flap.

| | |
|---|---|
| *What do you do in your free time? (formal)* | 暇な と 余は何をして いますか？ Nima na toki wa nani o shite imasuka |
| *What do you do in your free time? (informal)* | 暇な と 余は何 なに? hima na toki nani suru |
| *My hobby is reading.* | 趣味は読書です。 shumi wa dokusho desu |
| *I prefer the cinema.* | 私は映画の方が好き です。 watashi wa eiga no hogu sukidesu |
| *I hate opera.* | 私はオペラ大嫌い です。 watashi wa opera wa dakirai desu |

ゲームが好き
*gehmu ga suki*
*video games.*

俳優
*haiyu*
*actor*

舞台
*butai*
*stage*

**5  Say it**

I like music.

I prefer art.

My hobby is opera.

I hate theme parks.

**Read it**
These panels help you understand how the Japanese script works, present useful signs, and give tips for deciphering Japanese characters.

● **Read it**

空港  *kukoh*
     airport

Here's another example of two kanji characters combining to make a separate meaning: 空 (*ku*, "sky") + 港 (*koh*, "port")

**Say it**
In these exercises you are asked to apply what you have learned using different vocabulary.

**Dictionary**
A mini-dictionary provides ready reference from English to Japanese for 2,500 words.

**144** DICTIONARY

**Dictionary**
*English to Japanese*

The plural is usually the same as the singular in Japanese. In general, Japanese descriptive words, or adjectives, that change depending on how they are used. Some of these adjectives are followed by **(na)** or **(na)**. If a noun is used following such a word then the **na** or **na** must be put after the adjective: **kanojo wa kireh desu** (*she is pretty*); **kanojo wa kireh na joseih desu** (*she is a pretty girl*).

**A**

*(various dictionary entries in multiple columns)*

**B**

*(various dictionary entries)*

**Menu guide**
Use this guide as a reference for identifying popular Japanese dishes on the menu.

**128** MENU GUIDE

**Menu guide**

This guide lists the most common terms you may encounter on Japanese menus. Dishes are divided into categories and the Japanese script is displayed clearly to help you identify items on a menu.

### STARTERS AND SOUPS

| | | |
|---|---|---|
| hamu | ハム | *ham* |
| ohdoburu | オードブル | *hors d'oeuvres* |
| otsumami | おつまみ | *Japanese appetizer* |
| tsukidashi | つきだし | *Japanese appetizer* |
| he-ebi | 伊勢えび | *lobster* |
| meron | メロン | *melon* |
| minestorohne | ミネストローネ | *minestrone* |
| mashryon no | マッシュルームの | *mushroom soup* |
| kuruma-ebi | 車えび | *prawns* |
| smohku-sahmon | スモークサーモン | *smoked salmon* |
| misoshiru | みそ汁 | *soup with bean paste* |
| tomato su-pu | トマトスープ | *tomato soup* |

### EGG DISHES

| | | |
|---|---|---|
| behkon-eggu | ベーコンエッグ | *bacon and egg* |
| tamago | 卵 | *egg* |
| medama-yaki | 目玉焼き | *fried egg* |
| hamu-eggu | ハムエッグ | *ham and egg* |
| tamago-yaki | 玉子焼き | *Japanese omelette* |
| omuretsu | オムレツ | *omelette* |

**1    Warm up**

The Warm Up panel appears at the beginning of each topic. Use it to reinforce what you have already learned and to prepare yourself for moving ahead with the new subject.

# Konnichiwa
*Hello*

The Japanese bow is famous: the lower the bow, the more respectful. Traditionally, there would not be any contact in the form of a handshake or kisses. With the increasing Western influence, the Japanese now often shake hands, sometimes bowing at the same time, especially when meeting foreigners.

## 2    Words to remember

Say these expressions aloud. Hide the text on the left with the cover flap and try to remember the Japanese for each. Check your answers.

| | |
|---|---|
| おはようございます。<br>ohayo gozaimasu | *Good morning.* |
| こんばんは。<br>konbanwa | *Good evening.* |
| 私の名前は...です。<br>watashi no namae wa...desu | *My name is...* |
| どうぞ、よろしく。<br>dohzo yoroshiku | *Pleased to meet you.* |
| さようなら。<br>sayohnara | *Goodbye. (formal)* |
| さよなら。<br>sayonara | *Goodbye. (informal)* |
| ではまたあした。<br>dewa mata ashita | *See you tomorrow.* |

こんにちは。
konnichiwa
*Hello!*

## 3    In conversation: formal

こんにちは。
私の名前は岡田です。
konnichiwa. watashi no namae wa Okada desu

*Hello. My name is Okada.*

こんにちは。私の名前はロバート・バーカーです。
konnichiwa. watashi no namae wa Robahto Barker desu

*Hello. My name is Robert Barker.*

どうぞ、よろしく。
dohzo yoroshiku

*Pleased to meet you.*

## 4 Put into practice

Join in this conversation. Read the Japanese beside the pictures on the left and then follow the instructions to make your reply. Then test yourself by concealing the answers with the cover flap.

こんばんは。
konbanwa
*Good evening.*

Say: *Good evening.*

こんばんは。
konbanwa

私の名前は前田美樹
朗です。
watashi no namae wa
Maeda Mikiro desu
*My name is Maeda Mikiro.*

Say: *Pleased to meet you, Maeda-san.*

どうぞ、よろ
しく前田さん。
dohzo yoroshiku
Maeda-san

### ● Conversational tip The

Japanese usually introduce themselves using either just the family name – Okada – or the family name followed by the first name – Maeda Mikiro. But they are used to hearing Western names the other way: Robert Barker. It's not common to ask someone their name directly, so listen carefully to the introductions. When talking to/about others, you should add the honorific "san", but don't use "san" when talking about yourself. Levels of formality are inbuilt into the Japanese language and it takes time to acquire a feel for this. This programme will introduce you to polite, but not overformal, Japanese.

## 5 In conversation: informal

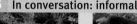

ではまたあした？
dewa mata ashita

*See you tomorrow?*

はい。ではまた
あした。
Hai, dewa mata ashita

*Yes, see you tomorrow.*

さよなら。
sayonara

*Goodbye.*

## 1 Warm up

Say "hello" and "goodbye" in Japanese. (pp.8–9)

Now say "My name is...". (pp.8–9)

Say "Pleased to meet you, Maeda-san". (pp.8–9)

# Watashi no kazoku
# *My family*

Japanese has two sets of vocabulary for family members, depending on whether you are talking about your own or someone else's. This lesson concentrates on talking about your own family. As **chichi** means *my father*, **musume** *my daughter*, etc., there is no need for a separate word meaning *my*.

## 2 Match and repeat

Look at the numbered family members in this scene and match them with the vocabulary list at the side. Read the Japanese words aloud. Now, hide the list with the cover flap and test yourself.

1 祖母
  sobo

2 祖父
  sofu

3 父
  chichi

4 母
  haha

5 息子
  musuko

6 娘
  musume

❶ *my grandmother*

❷ *my grandfather*

❸ *my father*

❻ *my daughter*

❹ *my mother*

❺ *my son*

🔊 **Conversational tip** Japanese distinguishes between "little" and "big" sister or brother. You will find all the relevant words in section 4. The word "kyohdai" (siblings) is used to refer to your brothers and sisters as a group: "kyohdai ga yo nin imasu" (I have four siblings).

## 3 Words to remember: numbers

Memorize these words and then test yourself using the cover flap.

The numbers opposite are "general" numerals used for mathematical functions or for money. The Japanese use a system of "classifiers" to count specific things. These vary with the nature of what is being counted, for example, its shape (long and thin, round and flat, etc.). A beginner can get away with using the general numbers, but it's useful to know the classifiers used for people to talk about your family:

一人 **hitori** 1 person
二人 **futari** 2 people
三人 **san nin** 3 people
四人 **yo nin** 4 people
五人 **go nin** 5 people
六人 **roku nin** 6 people
七人 **shichi nin** 7 people
八人 **hachi nin** 8 people
九人 **kyu nin** 9 people
十人 **jyu nin** 10 people

| | | |
|---|---|---|
| *one* | 一 | ichi |
| *two* | 二 | ni |
| *three* | 三 | san |
| *four* | 四 | shi/yon |
| *five* | 五 | go |
| *six* | 六 | roku |
| *seven* | 七 | shichi/nana |
| *eight* | 八 | hachi |
| *nine* | 九 | kyu |
| *ten* | 十 | jyu |
| *eleven* | 十一 | jyu-ichi |
| *twelve* | 十二 | jyu-ni |

## 4 Words to remember: relatives

Look at these words and say them aloud. Hide the text on the right with the cover flap and try to remember the Japanese. Check your answers and repeat, if necessary. Then practise the phrases below.

妻
tsuma
*my wife*

夫
otto
*my husband*

結婚しています。
kekkon shite imasu
*I'm married.*

| | | |
|---|---|---|
| *my big sister/ my little sister* | 姉/妹 | ane/imohto |
| *my big brother/ my little brother* | 兄/弟 | ani/otohto |
| *my siblings* | 兄弟 | kyohdai |
| *This is my wife.* | これは私の妻です。 | kore wa watashi no tsuma desu |
| *I have four children.* | 子供が四人います | kodomo ga yo nin imasu |
| *We have two daughters.* | 娘が二人います | musume ga futari imasu |

## 1 Warm up

Say the Japanese for as many members of (your own) family as you can. (pp.10–11)

Say "I have two sons". (pp.10–11)

# Shinseki
## *Your relatives*

Japanese has more respectful terms when referring to someone else's relatives. *Your mother* is **okahsan**; *your* is understood. Likewise, it's not common to use *his* or *her*, but to specify a name (+ **san**), for example, **kore wa Akiko-san no otohsan desu** *(This is her [Akiko's] father)*.

## 2 Words to remember

There are different words for referring to family members in Japanese. Here are the more respectful terms for someone else's family.

| | |
|---|---|
| お母さん<br>okahsan | *mother* |
| お父さん<br>otohsan | *father* |
| 息子さん<br>musuko san | *son* |
| 娘さん<br>musume san | *daughter* |
| 奥さん<br>okusan | *wife* |
| ご主人<br>goshujin | *husband* |
| 子供さん<br>kodomo san | *children* |
| ご兄弟<br>go kyohdai | *siblings* |

これはお母さん
ですか？
kore wa okahsan
desuka

*Is this your mother?*

## 3 In conversation

これはご主人ですか？
kore wa goshujin desuka

*Is this your husband?*

そうです。そして
これは私の父です。
sodesu. soshite kore wa
watashi no chichi desu

*That's right. And this
is my father.*

子供さんはいますか？
kodomo san wa
imasuka

*Do you have any
children?*

**◉ Conversational tip** Forming a question in Japanese is straightforward. Generally you add the question marker か "ka" to the end of a sentence: "a-re wa musuko san desu" (That's your son); "a-re wa musuko san desuka" (Is that your son?). In less formal spoken Japanese, the question marker is sometimes dropped "a-re wa musuko san".

## 4 Useful phrases

Read these phrases aloud several times and try to memorize them. Conceal the Japanese with the cover flap and test yourself.

| | | |
|---|---|---|
|  | *Do you have any siblings? (formal)* | ご兄弟はいらっしゃいますか？<br>go kyohdai wa irasshai masuka |
| | *Do you have any siblings? (informal)* | 兄弟いる？<br>kyohdai iru |
|  | *Is this your father?* | これはお父さんですか？<br>kore wa otohsan desuka |
| | *Is that your son? (formal)* | あれは息子さんですか？<br>a-re wa musuko san desuka |
|  | *This is Akiko's daughter.* | これは明子さんの娘さんです。<br>kore wa Akiko-san no musume san desu |
| | *Is that your little sister? (informal)* | あれは妹？<br>a-re wa imohto |

いいえ、でも妹がいます。
ihe, demo imohto ga imasu

*No, but I have a little sister.*

## 5 Say it

Is this your wife?

Is that your little brother?

Do you have a son? (informal)

This is Akiko's mother.

### 1 Warm up

Say "See you tomorrow". (pp.8–9)

Say "I'm married" (pp.10–11) and "Is this your wife?" (pp.12–13)

# Desu/ga arimasu
## *To be/there is*

The most common verb in Japanese is **desu**, meaning *is*, *are*, or *am*. The **u** is pronounced only slightly, often making it sound more like **dess**. **Desu** is placed at the end of a sentence and does not change depending on the subject (*I, you, he,* etc.): **watashi wa Robahto desu** *(I'm Robert)*.

## 2 Useful phrases with desu

Notice that you'll often find the marker は **wa** or あ **ga** after the subject of a sentence. The word order is: *subject* + **wa/ga** *(subject marker)* + *rest of sentence* + **desu**.

| | | |
|---|---|---|
| 私は日本人です。<br>watashi wa nihonjin desu | *I'm Japanese.* | |
| 今10時です。<br>ima jyuji desu | *It's ten o'clock.* | |
| あなたはお医者さんですか？<br>anata wa oisha san desuka | *Are you a doctor?* | |
| 明子さんは学生です。<br>Akiko-san wa gakusei desu | *Akiko is a student.* | |

---

🔘 **Read it** It's not as difficult to decipher Japanese script as it may at first appear. The most important thing to appreciate initially is that typical Japanese sentences consist of a mixture of three different character systems:

**1. Kanji:** Traditional Chinese characters imported into Japanese, e.g. 車 **kuruma** *(car)*, 母 **haha** *(my mother)*. **Kanji** represent an idea, rather than a particular sound.

**2. Hiragana:** Japanese characters representing syllables, e.g. で **de**, れ **re**. **Hiragana** is often used for "grammatical" words, e.g. です **desu** *(is)*, あれ **a-re** *(that)*.

**3. Katakana:** A second syllabary mainly used for foreign loan words, e.g. アメリカ **amerika** *(America)*, ケーキ **kehki** *(cake)*.

私はイギリス人です。
watashi wa igirisu jin desu
*I'm English.*

## 3 Useful phrases: talking about what you have

An informal and straightforward way to talk about what you have is to use the expression **(ga/wa) arimasu**, literally meaning *there is*. This changes to **(ga/wa) imasu** when talking about people rather than objects.

| | |
|---|---|
| *I have three children.* | 子供が三人います。<br>kodomo ga san nin imasu |
| *My son has a car.* | 息子には車があります。<br>musuko niwa kuruma ga arimasu |
| *I have a little sister.* | 妹がいます。<br>imohto ga imasu |
| *Do you have any children?* | 子供さんはいますか？<br>kodomo san wa imasuka |

名刺があります。
meishi ga arimasu
*I have a business card.*

## 4 Negatives

Negative sentences are made in different ways in Japanese, but sometimes use the negative phrase **arimasen**. Learn these phrases and then test yourself by concealing the answers with the cover flap.

| | |
|---|---|
| *We're not American.* | アメリカ人ではありません。<br>amerika jin dewa arimasen |
| *I don't have a car.* | 車がありません。<br>kuruma ga arimasen |

## 5 Put into practice

Join in this conversation. Read the Japanese beside the pictures on the left and then follow the instructions to make your reply. Then test yourself by concealing the answers with the cover flap.

こんばんは。
konbanwa
*Good evening.*

*Say: Good evening.
I'm Robert.*

こんばんは。
私はロバートです。
konbanwa. watashi wa Robahto desu

どうぞよろしく。
dohzo yoroshiku
*Pleased to meet you.*

*Say: I have a business card.*

名刺があります。
meishi ga arimasu

# Fukushu to kurikaeshi
*Review and repeat*

## Kotae
*Answers*
Cover with flap

### 1 How many?

1 三
san

2 九
kyu

3 四
shi/yon

4 二
ni

5 八
hachi

6 十
jyu

7 五
go

8 七
shichi/nana

9 六
roku

### 1 How many?

Hide the answers with the cover flap. Then say these Japanese numbers aloud. Check you have remembered the Japanese correctly.

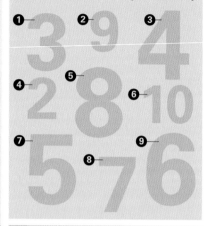

### 2 Hello

1 こんばんは。
私の名前は...です。
konbanwa.
watashi no namae
wa...desu

2 どうぞ、よろしく。
dohzo yoroshiku

3 息子が二人いま
す。子供さんは
いますか？
musuko ga futari
imasu. kodomo
san wa imasuka

4 さようなら
sayohnara

### 2 Hello

You meet someone in a formal situation. Join in the conversation, replying in Japanese following the English prompts.

konbanwa. watashi no namae wa Maeda
Mikiro desu
1 *Answer the greeting and give your name.*

kore wa watashi no tsuma desu
2 *Say "Pleased to meet you".*

kodomo san wa imasuka
3 *Say "I have two sons.*
*Do you have any children?"*

kodomo ga yo nin imasu
4 *Say "Goodbye." formally.*

## 3 Be or have

Fill in the blanks with **desu** (*to be*) or **arimasu/ imasu** (*"there is/are"* used to mean *"has/have"*). Then check you have remembered correctly.

1 watashi wa nihonjin
  \_\_\_\_

2 ani ga \_\_\_\_

3 anata wa gakusei san
  \_\_\_\_ ka

4 Sarah-san wa igirisu jin \_\_\_\_

5 watashi no namae wa Okada \_\_\_\_

6 meishi ga \_\_\_\_

7 kore wa watashi
  no otto \_\_\_\_

8 musume ga
  futari \_\_\_\_

### 3 Be or have

1 です
  desu

2 います
  imasu

3 です
  desu

4 です
  desu

5 です
  desu

6 あります
  arimasu

7 です
  desu

8 います
  imasu

## 4 Family

Say the Japanese for each of the numbered family members. Check you have remembered the Japanese correctly.

❶ *my grandmother*

❷ *my grandfather*

*my father* ❸

❹ *my daughter*   ❻ *my mother*

❺ *my son*

### 4 Family

1 祖母
  sobo

2 祖父
  sofu

3 父
  chichi

4 娘
  musume

5 息子
  musuko

6 母
  haha

# Kafe de
## *In the café*

<table>
<tr><td>

**1 Warm up**

Count up to ten.
(pp.10–11)

Remind yourself how
to say "hello" and
"goodbye". (pp.8–9)

Ask "Do you have
any children?"
(pp.14–15)

</td></tr>
</table>

You will find different types of cafés
in Japan: there are traditional cafés,
the most common of which is called
**an-mitsu kissa**; and Western-style
coffee houses, simply called **kafe** or
**kissaten**. These cafés are very popular,
particularly amongst younger Japanese.

[●] **Cultural tip** The generic Japanese word for
tea is "cha". In a regular café, Japanese green tea
would be called "ocha", "sencha" or "ryokucha".
Western-style tea is known as "kohcha" (red tea).

## 2 Words to remember

Look at the words below and say them out
loud a few times. Conceal the Japanese with
the cover flap and try to remember each one
in turn. Practise also the words on the right.

| | |
|---|---|
| ココア<br>kokoah | *hot chocolate* |
| ミルクティー<br>miruku tih | *tea with milk* |
| お茶<br>ocha | *(green) tea* |
| サンドイッチ<br>sando icchi | *sandwich* |

紅茶
kohcha
*(red) tea*

## 3 In conversation

コーヒーをお願い
します。
koh-hi o onegai shimasu

*A coffee, please.*

他にご注文は？
hoka ni gochumon wa

*Anything else?*

ケーキはありますか？
kehki wa arimasuka

*Do you have any
cakes?*

ケーキ
kehki
*cake*

砂糖
satoh
*sugar*

コーヒー
koh-hi
*coffee*

## 4 Useful phrases

Learn these phrases. Read the English under the pictures and say the phrase in Japanese as shown on the right. Then cover up the answers on the right and test yourself.

コーヒーをお願い
します。
koh-hi o onegai
shimasu

*A coffee, please.*

他にご注文は？
hoka ni gochumon wa

*Anything else?*

ケーキもお願い
します。
kehki mo onegai
shimasu

*A cake, too, please.*

いくらですか？
ikura desuka

*How much is that?*

はい、ございます。
hai, gozaimasu

*Yes, certainly.*

じゃケーキをお願い
します。いくら
ですか？
jya kehki o onegai
shimasu. ikura desuka

*Then I'd like a cake.
How much is that?*

８００円です。
happyaku yen desu

*That's 800 yen.*

## 1 Warm up

Say "A coffee, please".
(pp.18–19)

Say "I don't have a
car". (pp.14–15)

Ask "Do you have any
cakes?" (pp.18–19)

# Resutoran de
## *In the restaurant*

There are different types of eating
places in Japan. In a bar or café you
can find snacks or a light meal. A
**ryohteh** serves traditional Japanese
food. Department stores often house
relaxed **resutoran** on the upper floors,
open until about 10pm and serving
both international and Japanese dishes.

## 2 Words to remember

Familiarize yourself with these words and
test yourself using the flap.

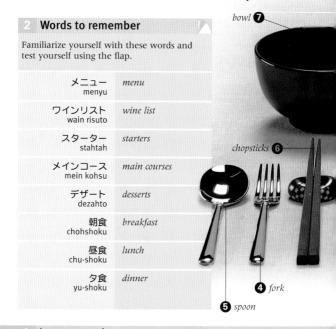

bowl **7**

| | |
|---|---|
| メニュー<br>menyu | *menu* |
| ワインリスト<br>wain risuto | *wine list* |
| スターター<br>stahtah | *starters* |
| メインコース<br>mein kohsu | *main courses* |
| デザート<br>dezahto | *desserts* |
| 朝食<br>chohshoku | *breakfast* |
| 昼食<br>chu-shoku | *lunch* |
| 夕食<br>yu-shoku | *dinner* |

chopsticks **6**

**4** fork

**5** spoon

## 3 In conversation

四人用のテーブルは
空いていますか？
yonin yoh no tehburu
wa aite imasuka

*Do you have a table
for four?*

予約なさってい
ますか？
yoyaku nasatte imasuka

*Do you have a
reservation?*

はい。バーカーで
予約しています。
hai. Barker de yoyaku
shite imasu

*Yes, in the name of
Barker.*

## 4  Match and repeat

Look at the numbered items in this table setting and match them with
the Japanese words on the right. Read the Japanese words aloud.
Now, conceal the Japanese with the cover flap and test yourself.

*glass* ❶

*hand towel* ❷

1 グラス
  gurasu

2 おしぼり
  oshibori

3 皿
  sara

4 フォーク
  forku

5 スプーン
  supuun

6 おはし
  ohashi

7 ボール
  bohru

## 5  Useful phrases

Practise these phrases and then test yourself
using the cover flap to conceal the Japanese.

| | |
|---|---|
| *What type of sushi do you have?* | どんな種類の寿司がありますか？<br>don-na shurui no sushi ga arimasuka |
| *Where can I pay?* | どこで払えますか？<br>doko de harae masuka |

*plate* ❸

喫煙席か禁煙席のど
ちらでしょうか？
kitsu-en seki ka kin-en
seki no dochira deshohka

*Would you like smoking
or non-smoking?*

禁煙席をお願い
します。
kin-en seki o onegai
shimasu

*Non-smoking, please.*

はい。こちらへどうぞ。
hai. kochira e dohzo

*Very well. Here you are.*

## 1  Warm up

Say "I'm married"
(pp.10–11) and "I'm
English". (pp.14–15)

Ask "Do you have any
siblings?" (pp.12–13)

Say "A sandwich,
please". (pp.18–19)

# Tabemono
*Dishes*

A typical meal in Japan would consist
of rice and miso soup, together with a
variety of fish, meat, and vegetable
dishes. The meal is served with pickles
and other condiments, such as ginger
and horseradish. Dessert is usually a
selection of fruit. Sweet puddings are
not very common.

**🔘 Cultural tip** In restaurants and food halls,
"tehshoku" (set menus) are popular, particularly at
lunchtime. These consist of a soup, rice, pickles, and
other dishes of your choice – all presented on a tray.

## 2  Match and repeat

Look at the numbered items and match them to the Japanese
words in the panel on the left.

1 果物
  kudamono

2 きのこ
  kinoko

3 米
  kome

4 野菜
  yasai

5 スープ
  supu

6 麺類
  men rui

7 魚
  sakana

8 肉
  niku

9 シーフード
  shifudo

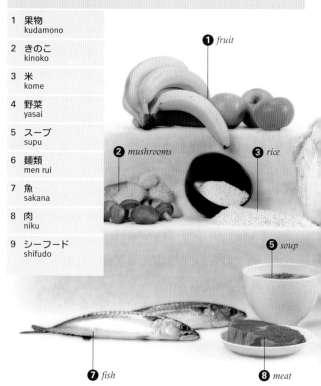

❶ *fruit*

❷ *mushrooms*

❸ *rice*

❺ *soup*

❼ *fish*

❽ *meat*

## 3 Words to remember: cooking methods

Familiarize yourself with these words.

| | | |
|---|---|---|
| *fried* | 揚げた | ageta |
| *grilled* | 焼いた | yaita |
| *roasted* | ロ!ーストした | rohsuto shita |
| *boiled* | ゆでた | yudeta |
| *steamed* | 蒸した | mushita |
| *raw* | 生の | nama no |

この魚は生のですか？
kono sakana wa nama
no desuka
*Is this fish raw?*

## 6 Say it

What's "Yakitori"?

A beer, please.

Is this fish grilled?

**4** *vegetables*

*noodles* **6**

**9** *seafood*

## 4 Words to remember: drinks

Familiarize yourself with these words.

| | | |
|---|---|---|
| *water* | 水 | mizu |
| *mineral water* | ミネラルウォーター | mineraru wohtah |
| *saki* | お酒 | osake |
| *wine* | ワイン | wain |
| *beer* | ビール | bihru |
| *fruit juice* | フルーツジュース | furutsu jyusu |

## 5 Useful phrases

Practise these phrases and then test yourself.

| | | |
|---|---|---|
| *I'm vegetarian.* | ベジタリアンです。 | bejitarian desu |
| *I'm allergic to nuts.* | ナッツ類でアレルギー反応を起こします。 | nattsu rui de arerugih. hannoh o okoshimasu |
| *What's "Chirinabe"?* | ちり鍋とは何ですか？ | chirinabe towa nan desuka |

## 1 Warm up

What are "breakfast", "lunch", and "dinner" in Japanese? (pp.20–1)

Say "I'm vegetarian" and "What's Sukiyaki?" in Japanese. (pp.22–3)

# Shite kudasai
## *Requests*

The simplest way to ask for something in Japanese is to say what you want, followed by **(o) onegai shimasu** *(please)*. You can use this in almost any situation. However, if you really want to impress, for example in a business situation, you could use the polite formula **itadake masuka**.

## 2 Basic requests

Here are some phrases using **(o) onegai shimasu** for making basic requests in Japanese. Learn these phrases and then test yourself by using the cover flap.

| | |
|---|---|
| 紅茶をお願いします。<br>kohcha o onegai shimasu | *(I'd like) some tea, please.* |
| ケーキをお願いします。<br>kehki o onegai shimasu | *(I'd like) a cake, please.* |
| フォークをお願いします。<br>forku o onegai shimasu | *(I'd like) a fork, please.* |
| ３人用のテーブルをお願いします。<br>san nin yoh no tehburu o onegai shimasu | *(I'd like) a table for for three, please.* |
| メニューをお願いします。<br>menyu o onegai shimasu | *(I'd like) the menu, please.* |
| キャンディをお願いします。<br>kyandih o onegai shimasu | *(I'd like) some sweets, please.* |
| 満タンでお願いします。<br>mantan de onegai shimasu | *Fill it up, please.* ("A full tank, please.") |

大和さんおねがいします。
Yamato-san onegai shimasu
*(I'd like) Mr Yamato, please.*

---

🔘 **Read it** Japanese "kanji" ideograms came from Chinese and are still used today. Some kanji are simple and resemble the item they describe, like the character for "people": 人(jin/nin), but many are quite intricate. The restaurant sign to the left is written in kanji. The three vertical characters say "jyun bi chu" ("preparation in progress") – a polite way of saying "closed"!

## 3 Polite requests

In a business situation, you may want to appear ultra-polite,
especially if you're talking to someone senior to yourself.
Learn these phrases and then test yourself by using the cover flap.

*Would you please
help me?*

手伝っていただけ
ますか？
tetsudatte itadake
masuka

*Could I have your
signature here,
please?*

ここにサインを
いただけますか？
koko ni sain o itadake
masuka

*Could I have your
phone number,
please?*

電話番号を教えて
いただけますか？
denwa bangoh o
oshiete itadake
masuka

## 4 Put into practice

Join in this conversation. Read the Japanese beside the pictures
on the left and then follow the instructions to make your reply
in Japanese. Test yourself by hiding the answers with the cover flap.

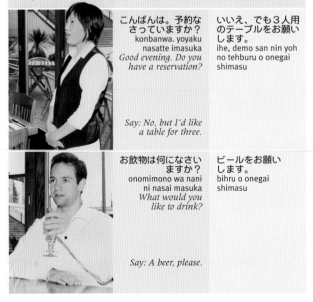

こんばんは。予約な
さっていますか？
konbanwa. yoyaku
nasatte imasuka
*Good evening. Do you
have a reservation?*

いいえ、でも3人用
のテーブルをお願い
します。
ihe, demo san nin yoh
no tehburu o onegai
shimasu

*Say: No, but I'd like
a table for three.*

お飲物は何になさい
ますか？
onomimono wa nani
ni nasai masuka
*What would you
like to drink?*

ビールをお願い
します。
bihru o onegai
shimasu

*Say: A beer, please.*

Kotae
*Answers*
Cover with flap

# Fukushu to kurikaeshi
*Review and repeat*

## 1 What food?

1 スープ
supu

2 野菜
yasai

3 魚
sakana

4 肉
niku

5 グラス
gurasu

6 米
kome

### 1 What food?

Name the numbered items.

❷ *vegetables*
❶ *soup*  ❸ *fish*
❹ *meat*
*glass* ❺

## 2 This is my...

1 これは私の夫
です。
kore wa watashi
no otto desu

2 これは私の娘
です。
kore wa watashi
no musume desu

3 これは私の兄弟
です。
kore wa watashi
no kyohdai desu

### 2 This is my...

Say these phrases in Japanese.

1 *This is my husband.*
2 *This is my daughter.*
3 *These are my siblings.*

## 3 I'd like...

1 ケーキをお願い
します。
kehki o onegai
shimasu

2 砂糖をお願い
します。
satoh o onegai
shimasu

3 コーヒーをお願
いします。
koh-hi o onegai
shimasu

4 紅茶をお願い
します。
kohcha o onegai
shimasu

### 3 I'd like...

Say "I'd like" the following:

*cake* ❶
❹ *tea*
*sugar* ❷
*coffee* ❸

**6** *rice*

*chopsticks* **7**

**8** *noodles*

*beer* **10**

**9** *hand towel*

## 1 What food?

7 おはし
ohashi

8 麺類
men rui

9 おしぼり
oshibori

10 ビール
bihru

## 4 Restaurant

You arrive at a restaurant. Join in the conversation, replying in Japanese where you see the English prompts.

konbanwa
1 *Ask "Do you have a table for three?"*

yoyaku nasatte imasuka
2 *Say "Yes, in the name of Barker"*

kitsu-en seki ka kin-en seki no dochira deshohka
3 *Say "Non-smoking, please".*

kochira no hoh e dohzo
4 *Say "The menu, please".*

mochiron gozaimasu
5 *Ask "Do you have a wine list?".*

## 4 Restaurant

1 3人用のテーブルは空いていますか？
san nin yoh no tehburu wa aite imasuka

2 はい。バーカーで予約しています。
hai. Barker de yoyaku shite imasu

3 禁煙席をお願いします。
kin-en seki o onegai shimasu

4 メニューをお願いします。
menyu o onegai shimasu

5 ワインリストはありますか？
wain risuto wa arimasuka

## 1 Warm up

How do you say
"I have four children"?
(pp.10–11)

Now say "We're not
English" and "I don't
have a car".
(pp.14–15)

What is Japanese
for "my mother"?
(pp.10–11)

# Hizuke to toshitsuki
## *Days and months*

The most important holiday of the
year in Japan is the three-day New
Year Holiday (**shohgatsu sanganichi**).
The Japanese usually spend this with
family. Christmas is also celebrated,
but more often spent with friends.

## 2 Words to remember: days of the week

Familiarize yourself with these words and test yourself using the flap.

| 月曜日<br>getsuyoh bi | *Monday* |
|---|---|
| 火曜日<br>kayoh bi | *Tuesday* |
| 水曜日<br>suiyoh bi | *Wednesday* |
| 木曜日<br>mokuyoh bi | *Thursday* |
| 金曜日<br>kin-yoh bi | *Friday* |
| 土曜日<br>doyoh bi | *Saturday* |
| 日曜日<br>nichiyoh bi | *Sunday* |
| 今日<br>kyoh | *today* |
| 明日<br>ashita | *tomorrow* |
| 昨日<br>kinoh | *yesterday* |

明日お会いしましょう。
ashita oai shimashoh
*We meet tomorrow.*

今日予約があります。
kyoh yoyaku ga arimasu
*I have a reservation
for today.*

## 3 Useful phrases: days

Learn these phrases and then test yourself using the cover flap.

| ミーティングは火曜<br>日ではありません。<br>mihtingu wa kayoh bi<br>dewa arimasen | *The meeting isn't<br>on Tuesday.* |
|---|---|
| 日曜日に仕事<br>をします。<br>nichiyoh bi ni shigoto<br>o shimasu | *I work on Sundays.* |

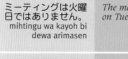

## 4 Words to remember: months of the year

Japanese months are named simply "1 month", "2 month", etc.

| | | |
|---|---|---|
| | *January* | 一月<br>ichi gatsu |
| | *February* | 二月<br>ni gatsu |
| | *March* | 三月<br>san gatsu |
| | *April* | 四月<br>shi gatsu |
| | *May* | 五月<br>go gatsu |
| | *June* | 六月<br>roku gatsu |
| | *July* | 七月<br>shichi gatsu |
| | *August* | 八月<br>hachi gatsu |
| | *September* | 九月<br>kyu gatsu |
| | *October* | 十月<br>jyu gatsu |
| | *November* | 十一月<br>jyu-ichi gatsu |
| | *December* | 十二月<br>jyu-ni gatsu |
| | *next month* | 来月<br>rai getsu |
| | *last month* | 先月<br>sen getsu |

私たちの記念日は
七月です。
watashi tachi no kinenbi
wa hichi gatsu desu
*Our anniversary is
in July.*

クリスマスは十二月
です。
kurisumasu wa jyu-ni
gatsu desu
*Christmas is in December.*

## 5 Useful phrases: months

Learn these phrases and then test yourself using the cover flap.

| | | |
|---|---|---|
| | *My children are on holiday in August.* | 子供たちは八月は休みです。<br>kodomo tachi wa hachi gatsu wa yasumi desu |
| | *My birthday is in June.* | 私の誕生日は六月です。<br>watashi no tanjyoh bi wa roku gatsu desu |

**1  Warm up**

Count in Japanese from one to twelve. (pp.10–11)

Say "Do you have a reservation?". (pp.20–1)

Say "The meeting isn't on Wednesday". (pp.28–9)

# Jikan to suhji
## Time and numbers

When telling the time in Japanese, the hour comes first, for example, **ichi ji** *(one o'clock)*, **ni ji** *(two o'clock)*, etc., following by the minutes: **go fun** *(five minutes)*, **jippun** *(ten minutes)*. **Mae** is added for times before the hour: **ni ji nippun mae** *(ten to two, literally "two o'clock ten minutes before")*.

## 2  Words to remember: time

Memorize how to tell the time in Japanese.

| | | |
|---|---|---|
| 1時<br>ichi ji | *one o'clock* | |
| 1時5分<br>ichi ji go fun | *five past one* | |
| 1時15分<br>ichi ji jyu-go fun | *quarter past one* | |
| 1時半<br>ichi ji han | *half past one* | |
| 1時20分<br>ichi ji nijyuppun | *twenty past one* | |
| 1時45分<br>ichi ji yonjyu-go fun | *quarter to two<br>("one forty-five")* | |
| 2時10分前<br>ni ji jippun mae | *ten to two* | |

## 3  Useful phrases

Learn these phrases and then test yourself using the cover flap.

| | |
|---|---|
| 今何時ですか？<br>ima nanji desuka | *What time is it?* |
| 朝食は何時がいいですか？<br>chohshoku wa nanji ga iidesuka | *At what time do you want breakfast?* |
| 12時に予約を入れています。<br>jyu-ni ji ni yoyaku o ireteimasu | *I have a reservation for twelve o'clock.* |

## 4 Words to remember: higher numbers

Japanese numbers are very logical. To count above ten, the individual numbers are simply added together. So 11 is **jyu-ichi** *("ten-one")*, 15 is **jyu-go** *("ten-five")*, etc. Be careful, though, to put the numbers the right way around: **go-jyu** is 50 *("five-ten")*, **nana-jyu** is 70 *("seven-ten")*. Units are added directly after the tens: 68 is **roku-jyu hachi**; 25 is **ni-jyu go**, and so on.

Pay special attention to the number 10,000, which is **man** or **ichi-man**. A million is **hyaku-man** *("one hundred-ten thousands")*.

五千円です。
go-sen yen desu
*That's 5000 yen.*

### 5 Say it

twenty-five

ninety-two

two hundred

twenty thousand

five to ten

half past eleven

That's 700 yen.

| | | |
|---|---|---|
| *eleven* | 十一 | jyu-ichi |
| *twelve* | 十二 | jyu-ni |
| *thirteen* | 十三 | jyu-san |
| *fourteen* | 十四 | jyu-shi/jyu-yon |
| *fifteen* | 十五 | jyu-go |
| *sixteen* | 十六 | jyu-roku |
| *seventeen* | 十七 | jyu-shichi |
| *eighteen* | 十八 | jyu-hachi |
| *nineteen* | 十九 | jyu-kyu |
| *twenty* | 二十 | ni-jyu |
| *thirty* | 三十 | san-jyu |
| *forty* | 四十 | yon-jyu |
| *fifty* | 五十 | go-jyu |
| *sixty* | 六十 | roku-jyu |
| *seventy* | 七十 | nana-jyu |
| *eighty* | 八十 | hachi-jyu |
| *ninety* | 九十 | kyu-jyu |
| *hundred* | 百 | hyaku |
| *three hundred* | 三百 | san-byaku |
| *thousand* | 千 | sen |
| *ten thousand* | 一万 | ichi-man |
| *two hundred thousand* | 二十万 | ni-jyu-man |
| *one million* | 百万 | hyaku-man |

# Apo/(go)yoyaku
*Appointments*

## 1 Warm up

Say the days of the week. (pp.28–9)

Say "three o'clock". (pp.30–1)

What's the Japanese for "today", "tomorrow", and "yesterday"? (pp.28–9)

The Japanese are keen to find out about the status of someone they meet for the first time. This is in order to judge the level of respect due and appropriate formality of the language. The most common way of establishing status is by the virtually obligatory exchange of business cards (**meishi**).

## 2 Useful phrases

Learn these phrases and then test yourself.

| 明日お会いしましょうか？<br>ashita oai shimashohka | *Shall we meet tomorrow?* |
|---|---|
| どなたとですか？<br>donata to desuka | *With whom? (formal)* |
| いつお暇ですか？<br>itsu ohima desuka | *When are you free?* |
| すみません。その日は忙しいです。<br>sumimasen. sonohi wa isogashih desu | *Sorry. I'm busy that day.* |
| 木曜日はどうですか？<br>mokuyoh bi wa doh desuka | *How about Thursday?* |
| 大丈夫です。<br>daijyohbu desu | *That's good for me.* |

ようこそ。
yohkoso
*Welcome.*

## 3 In conversation

こんにちは。アポを入れているのですが？
konnichiwa. apo o ireteiru no desuga

*Hello. I have an appointment.*

どなたとですか？
donata to desuka

*With whom?*

田中さんとです。
Tanaka-san to desu

*With Mr Tanaka.*

## 4 Put into practice

Practise these phrases. Then cover up the text on the right and say the answering part of the dialogue in Japanese. Check your answers and repeat if necessary.

| | | |
|---|---|---|
| | 木曜日にお会いしましょうか？<br>mokuyoh bi ni oai shimashohka<br>*Shall we meet on Thursday?*<br><br>Say: Sorry. I'm busy that day. | すみません。その日は忙しいです。<br>sumimasen. sonohi wa isogashih desu |
| | いつお暇ですか？<br>itsu ohima desuka<br>*When are you free?*<br><br>Say: On Tuesday in the afternoon. | 火曜日の午後なら空いています。<br>kayoh bi no gogo nara aite imasu |
| | 私も大丈夫です。<br>watashi mo daijyobu desu<br>*That's good for me, too.*<br><br>Ask: At what time? | 何時がよろしいですか？<br>nanji ga yoroshih desuka |

---

🔴 **Read it** It's useful to recognize some common Japanese signs you might see around a building. The signs below are a combination of two kanji characters. *Madoguchi* means literally "window mouth"!

 受付 *uketsuke* (reception)　　 窓口 *madoguchi* (information desk)

---

そうですか。何時のご予約ですか？
sohdesuka. nanji no goyoyaku desuka

*Very good. What time is the appointment?*

3時ですが。
san ji desuga

*At three o'clock.*

どうぞ、おかけください。
dohzo okake kudasai

*Take a seat, please.*

## 1 Warm up

How do you say "sorry"? (pp.32–3)

Ask "Shall we meet tomorrow?" (pp.32–3)

Say "(I'd like) a cake, please". (pp.24–5)

# Denwa de
## *On the telephone*

The Japanese answer the telephone with **moshi moshi** (*hello*), rather than **konnichiwa**. Public telephones are usually green. Almost all work with phonecards (**tereka**) available from most stores. International calls can be difficult from mobiles because of the different network specifications.

## 2 Match and repeat

Match the numbered items to the Japanese in the panel on the left and test yourself.

1 チャージャー
chahjyah

*charger* ❶

2 留守番電話
rusuban denwa

3 電話
denwa

❸ *telephone*

4 テレカ
tereka

5 携帯
kehtai

6 イヤフォン
iyafon

*earphones* ❻

❺ *mobile*

## 3 In conversation

もしもし、ジャパニーズコネクションです。
moshi moshi, japanihzu konekushon desu

*Hello? This is Japanese Connection.*

もしもし、岡田さんをお願いします。
moshi moshi, Okada-san o onegai shimasu

*Hello. (I'd like to speak to) Ms Okada, please.*

どちら様ですか？
dochira sama desuka

*Who's speaking?*

## 4 Useful phrases

Practise these phrases. Then test yourself using the cover flap.

Please connect me to
an outside line.

外線につなげて
ください。
gaisen ni tsunagete
kudasai

テレカをください。
tereka o kudasai
*I'd like a phonecard.*

(I'd like to speak to)
Mr/Ms Okada, please.

岡田さんをお願い
します。
Okada-san o onegai
shimasu

**2** answering
machine

Can I leave a
message?

メッセージを伝えて
いただけますか？
messehji o tsutaete
itadake masuka

**4** phonecard

Sorry, I have the
wrong number.

すみません、番号を
間違えました。
sumimasen, bangoh o
machigae mashita

ゴープレス・プリン
ターの前田美樹朗と
申します。
Gopress purintah no
Maeda Mikiro to
mohshimasu

*Maeda Mikiro of
Gopress Printers.*

すみません。ただ今
話し中です。
sumimasen. tadaima
hanashichu desu

*I'm sorry. The line is
busy.*

岡田さんの方から連
絡いただけますか？
Okada-san no hokara
renraku itadake masuka

*Can Ms Okada call me
back, please?*

<table><tr><td>

**Kotae**
*Answers*
Cover with flap

</td><td>

# Fukushu to kurikaeshi
*Review and repeat*

</td></tr></table>

## 1 Sums

1 十六
jyu-roku

2 三十九
san-jyu kyu

3 五十三
go-jyu san

4 七十八
nana-jyu hachi

5 九十九
kyu-jyu kyu

6 十七
jyu-hichi

## 1 Sums

Say the answers to these sums out loud in Japanese. Then check you have remembered correctly.

1 $10 + 6 = ?$

2 $14 + 25 = ?$

3 $66 - 13 = ?$

4 $40 + 38 = ?$

5 $90 + 9 = ?$

6 $20 - 3 = ?$

## 3 Telephones

What are the numbered items in Japanese?

*mobile* ❶

*phonecard* ❸

## 2 To want

1 します
shimasu

2 お願い
onegai

3 ますか
masuka

4 いただけ
itadake

5 お願い
onegai

6 人
nin

## 2 To want

Fill the gaps in these requests with the correct word.

1 Yamato-san onegai _____

2 kyandih o _____ shimasu

3 koko ni sain o itadake _____

4 tetsudatte _____ masuka

5 bihru o _____ shimasu

6 san _____ yoh no tehburu o onegai shimasu

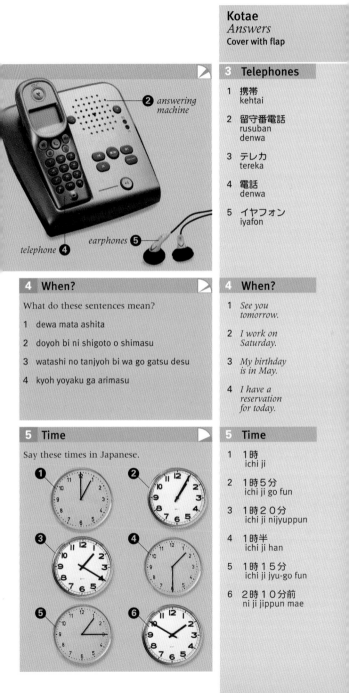

*answering machine* **2**

*telephone* **4**

*earphones* **5**

### 3 Telephones

1 携帯
kehtai

2 留守番電話
rusuban denwa

3 テレカ
tereka

4 電話
denwa

5 イヤフォン
iyafon

### 4 When?

What do these sentences mean?

1 dewa mata ashita

2 doyoh bi ni shigoto o shimasu

3 watashi no tanjyoh bi wa go gatsu desu

4 kyoh yoyaku ga arimasu

### 4 When?

1 *See you tomorrow.*

2 *I work on Saturday.*

3 *My birthday is in May.*

4 *I have a reservation for today.*

### 5 Time

Say these times in Japanese.

### 5 Time

1 1時
ichi ji

2 1時5分
ichi ji go fun

3 1時20分
ichi ji nijyuppun

4 1時半
ichi ji han

5 1時15分
ichi ji jyu-go fun

6 2時10分前
ni ji jippun mae

## 1 Warm up

Count to 100 in tens.
(pp.10–11 and
pp.30–1)

Ask "What time is it?"
(pp.30–1)

Say "half past one".
(pp.30–1)

# Eki de
## *At the station*

Japan is famous for its clean, fast, and
reliable train services. The network
covers the entire country and there
are different types of train: local **futsu**
and **kaisoku** commuter trains, **kyuko**
and **tokkyu** express trains; and the
famous **shinkansen** high-speed
intercity "bullet" trains.

## 2 Words to remember

Learn these words and then test yourself.

| | |
|---|---|
| 駅<br>eki | *station* |
| 電車<br>densha | *train* |
| プラットホーム<br>purattohohmu | *platform* |
| チケット<br>chiketto | *ticket* |
| 片道<br>katamichi | *single* |
| 往復<br>ohfuku | *return* |
| 一等 / 二等車<br>ittoh/nitoh sha | *first/second class* |
| 乗り換え<br>norikae | *change (trains)* |

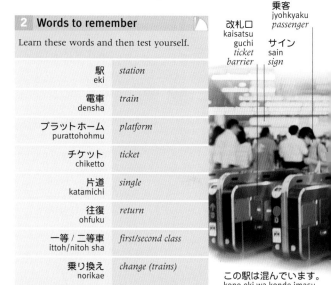

乗客
jyohkyaku
*passenger*

改札口
kaisatsu
guchi
*ticket
barrier*

サイン
sain
*sign*

この駅は混んでいます。
kono eki wa konde imasu
*This station is crowded.*

## 3 In conversation

京都行きを二枚おね
がいします。
Kyoto iki o nimai onegai
shimasu

*Two to Kyoto, please.*

往復ですか？
ohfuku desuka

*Is that return?*

はい。席の予約が
必要ですか？
hai. seki no yoyaku ga
hitsuyo desuka

*Yes. Do I need to make
seat reservations?*

## 4  Useful phrases

Learn these phrases and then test yourself using the cover flap.

大阪への電車は
遅れています。
Osaka eno densha wa
okurete imasu
*The train for Osaka
is late.*

| | |
|---|---|
| *How much is a ticket to Nagasaki?* | 長崎行きのチケットはいくらですか？<br>Nagasaki iki no chiketto wa ikura desuka |
| *Can I use a credit card?* | クレジットカードが使えますか？<br>kurejitto kahdo ga tsukae masuka |
| *Do I have to change?* | 乗り換えしなければいけませんか？<br>norikae shinakereba ikemasenka |
| *Which platform does the train leave from?* | 電車はどのプラットホームから発車しますか？<br>densha wa dono purattohohmu kara hassha shimasuka |
| *What time does the train leave?* | 電車は何時に発車しますか？<br>densha wa nanji ni hassha shimasuka |

## 5  Say it

This train is crowded.

How much is a ticket to Osaka?

**◉ Cultural tip** You might need to buy your rail tickets from machines. These machines can be complicated to navigate and you may need someone to help you. But all the destinations are written in phonetic katakana characters, as well as kanji, to help children (and foreigners) to read the signs.

いいえ。一万円になります。
ihe. ichiman-yen ni narimasu

*No. That's 10,000 yen.*

クレジットカードが使えますか？
kurejitto kahdo ga tsukae masuka

*Can I use a credit card?*

はい。電車はプラットホーム1番から発車します。
hai. densha wa purattohohmu ichiban kara hassha shimasu

*Yes. The train leaves from platform one.*

### 1    Warm up

How do you say
"train"? (pp.38–9)

What are "tomorrow"
and "yesterday" in
Japanese? (pp.28–9)

Count from 10 to 20.
(pp.30–1)

# Iku/noru
## *To go and to take*

**Iku** (*to go*) and **noru** (*to take*) are essential verbs you will need as you find your way around. Japanese verbs do not change according to the subject, but do have different endings for the *tense* (present/past) or *mood* (requesting/ wanting, etc.). Note also that the verb usually comes at the *end* of a sentence.

### 2    Iku/noru: to go and to take

The basic verb (**iku/noru**) can be used by itself, but often an ending is added. The present tense of Japanese verbs generally ends in **-masu**: ikimasu *(go, am/are/is going)* and the negative in **-masen**: ikemasen *(don't go, am not/aren't/isn't going)*. The "wanting" mood ends in **-tai**: noritai *(want to take)*.

| | |
|---|---|
| どこ行くの？<br>doko iku no | *Where are you going? (informal)* |
| どこに行かれるの<br>ですか？<br>doko ni ikareru no<br>desuka | *Where are you going? (formal)* |
| 今日は自転車に<br>乗ります。<br>kyoh wa jitensha ni<br>norimasu | *I'm taking my bicycle today.* |
| バスで仕事に<br>行きます。<br>basu de shigoto ni<br>ikimasu | *I go to work by bus.* |
| タクシーでは仕事に<br>行きません。<br>takushih dewa<br>shigotoni ikimasen | *I don't go to work by taxi.* |
| 電車に乗りたい<br>です。<br>densha ni noritai desu | *I want to take the train.* |

富士山に行きます。
fujisan ni ikimasu
*I'm going to Mount Fuji.*

**🔲 Cultural tip** Taxis in Japan are often yellow or green. There's usually a light at the bottom right of the windscreen: green for occupied and red for available. The taxis are usually scrupulously clean – drivers even wear white gloves. Back doors are remote controlled by the driver, so be careful you don't get knocked over as you reach for the handle. Tips are not usual.

## 3 Past and future

The ending **-mashita** shows a verb is in the past: **norimashita** *(took)*, **ikimashita** *(went)*. There is no special form for the future. Instead, the present tense can be used with a time indicator, e.g. **ashita** *(tomorrow)*.

| | |
|---|---|
| *I took a taxi.* | タクシーに乗り<br>ました。<br>takushih ni<br>norimashita |
| *I went to Mount Fuji<br>by train.* | 富士山に電車で行き<br>ました。<br>fujisan ni densha de<br>ikimashita |
| *I'll take the<br>underground<br>tomorrow.* | 明日地下鉄に<br>乗ります。<br>ashita chikatetsu ni<br>norimasu |
| *I'll go to work by bus<br>tomorrow.* | 明日バスで仕事に行<br>きます。<br>ashita basu de shigoto<br>ni ikimasu |

## 4 Put into practice

Cover the text on the right and complete the dialogue in Japanese.

どこに行かれるの<br>ですか？<br>doko ni ikareru no<br>desuka<br>*Where are you going?*

*Say: I'm going to the<br>station.*

駅に行きます。<br>eki ni ikimasu

地下鉄に乗りたい<br>ですか？<br>chikatetsu ni noritai<br>desuka<br>*Do you want to take<br>the underground?*

*Say: No, I want to<br>take the bus.*

いいえ、バスに乗り<br>たいです。<br>ihe, basu ni noritai<br>desu

三十四番のバス<br>ですよ。<br>san-jyu yon ban no<br>basu desuyo<br>*That'll be bus<br>number 34.*

*Say: Thank you very<br>much.*

どうもありがとう<br>ございます。<br>dohmo arigatoh<br>gozaimasu

Say "I want to go
to the station".
(pp.40–1)

Ask "Where are you
going?" (pp.40–1)

What's 45 in
Japanese? (pp.30–31)

# Takushih, basu, chikatetsu
## *Taxi, bus, and underground*

On buses you generally take a ticket
from a machine as you get on. At the
end of your journey, a chart will
indicate how much you have to pay.

## 2 Words to remember

Familiarize yourself with these words.

| | |
|---|---|
| バス<br>basu | *bus* |
| タクシー<br>takushih | *taxi* |
| 地下鉄<br>chikatetsu | *underground* |
| バス停<br>basu teh | *bus station* |
| タクシー乗り場<br>takushih noriba | *taxi rank* |
| 地下鉄の駅<br>chikatetsu no eki | *underground station* |
| 運賃<br>unchin | *fare* |
| 線<br>sen | *line/route* |

88番のバスはここで
停まりますか？
hachijyu-hachi ban no basu
wa kokode tomarimasuka
*Does the number 88 stop
here?*

## 3 In conversation: taxi

秋葉原までお願い
します。
Akihabara ma-de onegai
shimasu

*To Akihabara, please.*

わかりました。
wakarimashita

*Very well.*

ここで降ろして
ください。
kokode oroshite kudasai

*Can you drop me here,
please?*

## 4  Useful phrases

Learn these phrases and then test yourself using the cover flap.

| *A taxi to Ginza, please.* | 銀座までのタクシーをお願いします。<br>Ginza ma-de no takushih o onegai shimasu |

| *What time is the next bus to the airport?* | 空港行きの次のバスは何時ですか？<br>ku-koh iki no tsugi no basu wa nanji desuka |

| *How do you get to Asakusa?* | 浅草にはどうやって行けばいいですか？<br>Asakusa niwa dohyatte ikeba iidesuka |

| *Please wait for me.* | ちょっと待ってください。<br>chotto matte kudasai |

**● Cultural tip** Tokyo, Osaka, and other major cities have extensive and efficient metro systems. The different lines ("sen") have names such as "yamanote-sen" (a circular line which links the network). Fares vary depending on distance.

東京メトロ
Tokyo Metro

## 6  Say it

To the station, please.

A taxi to the airport, please.

How do you get to Akihabara?

## 5  In conversation: bus

博物館へ行きますか？
hakubutsu kan e ikimasuka

*Do you go to the museum?*

はい。あまり遠くないですよ。
hai. amari tohku naidesuyo

*Yes. It's not very far.*

どこでおりるか教えてもらえますか？
doko de oriru ka oshiete mora-e masuka

*Can you tell me when to get off?*

# Dohro de
## *On the road*

**1** Warm up

How do you say "A coffee, please"? (pp.14–15)

Say "my father", "my sister", and "my parents". (pp.12–13)

Say "I'm going to Ginza". (pp.40–1)

**Gairaigo** is a special term used to refer to the many foreign words imported into Japanese, mainly from English. In some areas of life, such as modern machinery and computers, **gairaigo** is dominant. Pay attention, though, to the particularly Japanese way of pronouncing the words.

## **2** Match and repeat

Match the numbered items to the list on the left, then test yourself.

1 フロントガラス
furonto garasu

2 ボンネット
bonn-netto

3 バンパー
banpah

4 タイヤ
taiya

5 ヘッドライト
heddo raito

6 ドア
doa

7 車輪
shahrin

8 トランク
toranku

9 サイドミラー
saido mirah

◉ **Cultural tip** Japan is one of the few countries that drives on the left, as does the UK. Many motorways are toll roads and can be expensive.

**①** *windscreen*

**②** *bonnet*

**③** *bumper*

**④** *tyre*

**⑤** *headlights*

## **3** Road signs

一方通行
ippoh tsu-koh

*One way*

徐行
jyokoh

*Proceed slowly*

最低速度
saiteh sokudo

*Minimum speed limit*

## 4  Useful phrases

Learn these phrases and then test yourself using the cover flap.

*The engine won't start.*

エンジンがかかり
ません。
enjin ga kakari masen

*Fill it up, please.*
("A full tank, please.")

満タンお願い
します。
mantan onegai shimasu

## 5  Words to remember

Familiarize yourself with these words then test yourself using the flap.

## 6  Say it

Diesel, please.

The car won't start.

| | | |
|---|---|---|
| *driving licence* | 運転免許証 | unten menkyosho |
| *petrol* | ガソリン | gasorin |
| *diesel* | ディーゼル | dihzeru |
| *oil* | オイル | oiru |
| *engine* | エンジン | enjin |
| *flat tyre* | パンク | panku |

**9** *wing mirror*

**8** *boot*

**6** *door*   **7** *wheel*

**Read it** Road signs are often in Japanese characters only. If you're driving, familiarize yourself with the Japanese script for your destination, as well as the more common signs, such as 止まれ **tomare** ("stop").

止まれ
tomare
*Stop*

進入禁止
shin-nyu kinshi
*No entry*

駐車禁止
chu-sha kinshi
*No parking*

# Fukushu to kurikaeshi
## *Review and repeat*

### 1 Transport

1 バス
 basu

2 タクシー
 takushih

3 車
 kuruma

4 自転車
 jitensha

5 地下鉄
 chikatetsu

### 1 Transport

Name these forms of transport
in Japanese.

bus **1**

taxi **2**

### 2 Go and take

1 行きます
 ikimasu

2 乗りたい
 noritai

3 行く
 iku

4 行かれる
 ikareru

5 乗ります
 norimasu

6 乗りました
 norimashita

### 2 Go and take

Use the correct form of the verb in brackets
to fill the gaps.

1 fujisan ni ____ (iku)

2 densha ni ____ desu (noru)

3 doko ____ no (iku)

4 doko ni ____ no desuka
 (iku)

5 ashita chikatetsu ni ____
 (noru)

6 kinoh takushih ni ____
 (noru)

**Kotae**
*Answers*
Cover with flap

**3** car

**4** bicycle

underground **5**

東京メトロ
Tokyo Metro

## 3 Questions

How do you ask
these questions in
Japanese?

1 *"Do you have any
cakes?"*

2 *"Do you have any
children?"*

3 *"What time is
it?"*

4 *"Do you go to the
station?"*

5 *"Where are you
going?"*
*(informal).*

6 *"Can I use a
credit card?"*

## 3 Questions

1 ケーキはあ
りますか？
kehki wa
arimasuka

2 子供さんは
いますか？
kodomo san wa
imasuka

3 今何時ですか？
ima nanji desuka

4 駅へ行きます
か？
eki e ikimasuka

5 どこ行くの？
doko iku no

6 クレジットカード
が使えますか？
kurejitto kahdo
ga tsukae
masuka

## 4 Tickets

You're buying tickets at a train station.
Join in the conversation, replying in Japanese
following the numbered English prompts.

konnichiwa
1 *Two to Osaka, please.*

ohfuku desuka
2 *No. Single, please.*

ichiman-yen ni narimasu
3 *What time does the train leave?*

ni ji jippun mae desu
4 *Which platform does the train
leave from?*

purattohohmu wa
ichiban desu
5 *Thank you
very much.*

## 4 Tickets

1 大阪行きを二枚
お願いします。
Osaka iki o nimai
onegai shimasu

2 いいえ。片道を
お願いします。
ihe. katamichi o
onegai shimasu

3 電車は何時に発
車しますか？
densha wa nanji
ni hassha
shimasuka

4 電車はどのプラ
ットホームから
発車しますか？
densha wa dono
purattohohmu
kara hassha
shimasuka

5 どうもありがと
うございます。
dohmo arigato
gozaimasu

## 1 Warm up

Ask "Do you go to the museum?" (pp.42–3)

What are "station" and "ticket" in Japanese? (pp.38–9)

# Machi de
## *About town*

To talk about features or facilities, you can use the phrases **ga/wa arimasu** (*there is/are*) and **ga/wa arimasen** (*there isn't/ aren't*). Notice the word order is the opposite to English: **hashi no chikaku ni suimingu pu-ru ga arimasu** = *bridge/near to/swimming pool/there is* (*There's a swimming pool near the bridge*).

## 2 Match and repeat

Match the numbered locations to the words in the panel.

1 横断歩道
ohdan hodoh

2 橋
hashi

3 デパート
depahto

4 駐車場
chusha jyo

5 噴水
funsui

6 広場
hiroba

7 博物館
hakubutsu kan

8 映画館
eiga kan

❶ crossing

*department* ❸
*store*

❷ bridge

❽ cinema

## 3 Words to remember

Familiarize yourself with these words and test yourself using the cover flap.

| | |
|---|---|
| ガソリンスタンド<br>gasorin sutando | *petrol station* |
| 観光案内所<br>kankoh an-naijyo | *tourist information centre* |
| スイミングプール<br>suimingu pu-ru | *swimming pool* |
| ネットカフェ<br>netto kafeh | *internet café* |

## 4 Useful phrases

Learn these phrases and then test yourself using the cover flap.

| | |
|---|---|
| *Is there a museum in town?* | 街に博物館があり ますか？<br>machi ni hakubutsu kan ga arimasuka |
| *Is it far from here?* | ここから遠いですか？<br>koko kara toh-i desuka |
| *There's a swimming pool near the bridge.* | 橋の近くにスイミン グプールがあります。<br>hashi no chikaku ni suimingu pu-ru ga arimasu |
| *There isn't a tourist information centre.* | 観光案内所はありま せん。<br>kankoh an-naijyo wa arimasen |

寺は街の真ん中にあ ります。
tera wa machi no man-naka ni arimasu
*The temple is in the centre of town.*

## 5 Put into practice

Join in this conversation. Read the Japanese on the left and follow the instructions to make your reply. Then test yourself by concealing the answers with the cover flap.

| | |
|---|---|
| どうしました？<br>doh shimashita<br>*Is everything OK?* | この近くにネットカ フェはありますか？<br>kono chikaku ni netto kafe wa arimasuka |
| *Ask: Is there an internet café nearby?* | |
| いいえ、でも観光案 内所はあります。<br>ihe, demo kankoh an-naijyo wa arimasu<br>*No, but there's a tourist information centre.* | ここから遠い ですか？<br>koko kara toh-i desuka |
| *Ask: Is it far from here?* | |
| 駅の近くです。<br>eki no chikaku desu<br>*It's near the station.* | ありがとうござい ます。<br>arigatoh gozaimasu |
| *Say: Thank you.* | |

**4** car park

**5** fountain

**6** square

**7** museum

## 1 Warm up

How do you say "bridge" and "fountain"? (pp.48–9)

Ask "Is it far from here?" (pp.48–9)

Ask "Is there a museum in town?" (pp.48–9)

# Michi o kiku
## *Asking directions*

Finding your way around town in Japan can be confusing, so it's a good idea to learn how to ask for and understand directions. Remember that Japanese word order is different from English: **kado o hidari ni magette kudasai** = *corner at/left towards/turn/please* ("Turn left at the corner").

## 2 Useful phrases

Practise these phrases and then test yourself.

| | |
|---|---|
| 左 / 右に曲がってください。<br>hidari/migi ni magatte kudasai | *(Please) turn left/right.* |
| 左に / 右に<br>hidari ni/migi ni | *On the left/on the right* |
| まっすぐ<br>massugu | *Straight on* |
| 寺にはどうやって行けばいいですか？<br>tera niwa dohyatte ikeba iidesuka | *How do I get to the temple?* |
| 左側の最初の道<br>hidari gawa no saisho no michi | *First street on the left* |
| 右の二番目の道<br>migi no ni-banme no michi | *Second street on the right* |

オフィスブロック
ofisu burokku
*office block*

公園
kohen
*park*

角を左に曲がってください
kado o hidari ni magatte kudasai
*Turn left at the corner.*

## 3 In conversation

この街にレストランはありますか？
kono machi ni resutoran wa arimasuka

*Is there a restaurant in town?*

はい。駅の近くにあります。
hai. eki no chikaku ni arimasu

*Yes, near the station.*

駅にはどうやって行けばいいですか？
eki niwa dohyatte ikeba iidesuka

*How do I get to the station?*

## 4 Words to remember

Familiarize yourself with these words and test yourself using the flap.

道に迷いました。
michi ni mayoi mashita
*I'm lost.*

| | | |
|---|---|---|
| *traffic lights* | 信号 | shingoh |
| *corner* | 角 | kado |
| *street* | 道 | michi |
| *road* | 道路 | dohro |
| *map* | 地図 | chizu |
| *flyover* | 立体交差 | rittai kohsa |
| *opposite* | 反対側 | hantai gawa |
| *at the end of the street* | 道の終わりに | michi no owari ni |

ここはどこですか？
koko wa doko desuka
*Where are we?*

## 5 Say it

Turn right at the traffic lights.

Turn left at the station.

It's about ten minutes.

信号を左に曲がってください。
shingoh o hidari ni magatte kudasai

*Turn left at the traffic lights.*

遠いですか？
toh-i desuka

*Is it far?*

いいえ、5分くらいです。
ihe, go fun kurai desu

*No, it's about five minutes.*

## 1 Warm up

Say the days of the week in Japanese. (pp.28–9)

How do you say "six o'clock"? (pp.30–1)

Ask "What time is it?" (pp.30–1)

# Kankoh
## *Sightseeing*

Japanese shops open late, closing around 10 or 11pm. The main closing days for tourist sights are Sunday or Monday. However, urban Japan is a 24/7 society and you will generally find a few **konbini** (abbreviated from "convenience stores") and cafés open whatever the time of day or night.

## 2 Words to remember

Familiarize yourself with these words and test yourself using the flap.

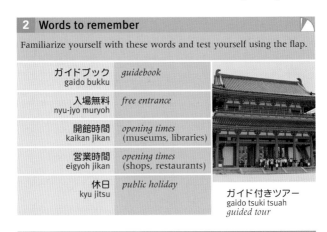

| ガイドブック<br>gaido bukku | *guidebook* |
|---|---|
| 入場無料<br>nyu-jyo muryoh | *free entrance* |
| 開館時間<br>kaikan jikan | *opening times*<br>(museums, libraries) |
| 営業時間<br>eigyoh jikan | *opening times*<br>(shops, restaurants) |
| 休日<br>kyu jitsu | *public holiday* |

ガイド付きツアー
gaido tsuki tsuah
*guided tour*

> 🔘 **Cultural tip** There are many unusual free attractions in Japan. These include beer, sake, and fishcake museums, wine cellars, food factories, galleries, electronics and cosmetics showrooms, and even television and film studios.

## 3 In conversation

今日の午後は開いていますか？
kyoh no koko wa aite imasuka

*Do you open this afternoon?*

はい、でも六時には閉まります。
hai, demo roku ji niwa shimari masu

*Yes, but we close at six o'clock.*

車いすは使えますか？
kurumaisu wa tsukae masuka

*Is wheelchair access possible?*

## 4 Useful phrases

Learn these phrases and then test yourself using the cover flap.

| | |
|---|---|
| *What time do you open?* | 何時に開きますか？<br>nanji ni akimasuka |
| *What time does the shop close?* | 店は何時に閉まり<br>ますか？<br>mise wa nanji ni<br>shimari masuka |
| *Is wheelchair access possible?* | 車いすは使えます<br>か？<br>kurumaisu wa tsukae<br>masuka |

## 5 Put into practice

Cover the text on the right and complete the dialogue in Japanese.

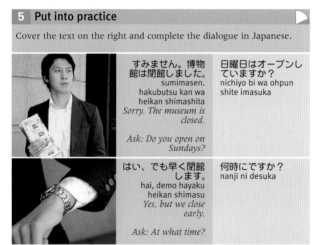

すみません。博物
館は閉館しました。
sumimasen.
hakubutsu kan wa
heikan shimashita
*Sorry. The museum is
closed.*

*Ask: Do you open on
Sundays?*

日曜日はオープンし
ていますか？
nichiyo bi wa ohpun
shite imasuka

はい、でも早く閉館
します。
hai, demo hayaku
heikan shimasu
*Yes, but we close
early.*

*Ask: At what time?*

何時にですか？
nanji ni desuka

はい。あちらにエレ
ベーターがあります。
hai. achira ni erebehtah
ga arimasu

*Yes, there's a lift over
there.*

ありがとう。
チケットを四枚お願
いします。
arigatoh. chiketto o
yonmai onegai shimasu

*Thank you. I'd like
four tickets.*

どうぞ。ガイドブックは
無料です。
dohzo. gaido bukku wa
muryoh desu

*Here you are. The
guidebook is free.*

## 1 Warm up

Say "Would you please help me?". (pp.24–5)

What's the Japanese for "ticket"? (pp.38–9)

Say "I'm going to Osaka". (pp.40–1)

# Ku-koh de
## *At the airport*

International flights arrive at Tokyo's Narita airport and an extensive network of internal flights operate out of the domestic Haneda airport. Although the airport environment is largely universal, it is sometimes useful to be able to understand key words and phrases in Japanese.

## 2 Words to remember

Familiarize yourself with these words and test yourself using the flap.

| チェックイン<br>chekku in | *check-in* |
| 出発<br>shuppatsu | *departures* |
| 到着<br>tohchaku | *arrivals* |
| 税関<br>zeikan | *customs* |
| 入国審査／出国審査<br>nyu-koku shinsa/<br>shukkoku shinsa | *passport control*<br>*(entering/leaving*<br>*Japan)* |
| ターミナル<br>tahminaru | *terminal* |
| 搭乗口<br>tohjyoh guchi | *gate* |
| …便<br>bin | *flight number…* |

香港行きの飛行機はど
この搭乗口ですか？
honkon iki no hikohki
wa doko no tohjyoh
guchi desuka
*Which gate is the flight*
*to Hong Kong?*

## 3 Useful phrases

Learn these phrases and then test yourself using the cover flap.

| ロンドンからの飛行機<br>は予定通りですか？<br>Rondon kara no hikohki<br>wa yotei dohri desuka | *Is the flight from*<br>*London on time?* |
| 荷物が見つかり<br>ません。<br>nimotsu ga mitsukari<br>masen | *I can't find my*<br>*baggage.* |
| 京都への飛行機は<br>遅れています。<br>Kyoto eno hikohki wa<br>okurete imasu | *The flight to Kyoto*<br>*is delayed.* |

## 4 Put into practice

Join in this conversation. Read the Japanese on the left and follow the instructions to make your reply. Then test yourself by concealing the answers with the cover flap.

次の方どうぞ。
tsugi no kata dohzo
*Next, please.*

*Ask: Is the flight to Kyoto on time?*

京都への飛行機は予定通りですか?
Kyoto eno hikohki wa yotei dohri desuka

はい。予定通りです。
hai. yotei dohri desu
*Yes, it's on time.*

*Ask: Which gate is it?*

どの搭乗口ですか?
dono tohjyoh guchi desuka

## 5 Match and repeat

Match the numbered items to the Japanese words in the panel.

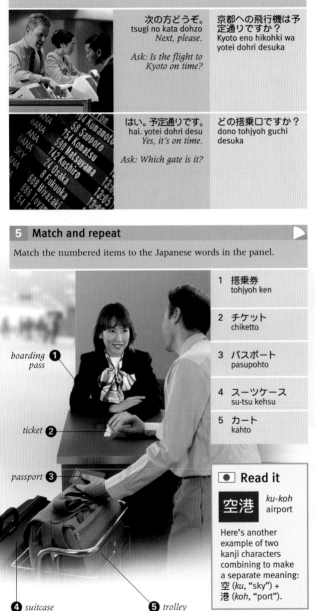

*boarding pass* ❶

*ticket* ❷

*passport* ❸

❹ *suitcase*

❺ *trolley*

1 搭乗券
tohjyoh ken

2 チケット
chiketto

3 パスポート
pasupohto

4 スーツケース
su-tsu kehsu

5 カート
kahto

### ● Read it

空港 *ku-koh* airport

Here's another example of two kanji characters combining to make a separate meaning: 空 (*ku*, "sky") + 港 (*koh*, "port").

# Fukushu to kurikeshi
*Review and repeat*

**Kotae**
*Answers*
Cover with flap

## 1 Places

1 博物館
hakubutsu kan

2 横断歩道
ohdan hodoh

3 橋
hashi

4 寺
tera

5 駐車場
chusha jyo

6 デパート
tepahto

7 広場
hiroba

## 1 Places

Name the numbered places in Japanese.

**1** *museum*  **2** *crossing*  **3** *bridge*

**4** *temple*  **5** *car park*

**6** *department store*

**7** *square*

## 2 Car parts

1 フロントガラス
furonto
garasu

2 ヘッドライト
heddo
raito

3 バンパー
banpah

4 ドア
doa

5 タイヤ
taiya

## 2 Car parts

Name these car parts in Japanese.

*windscreen* **1**

**5** *tyre*  *door* **4**

## 3 Translation

What do these Japanese phrases mean?

1 hidari ni magatte kudasai

2 kono machi ni hakubutsu kan wa arimasuka

3 mantan de onegai shimasu

4 koko wa doko desuka

5 hashi no chikaku ni suimingu puhru ga arimasu

6 nanji ni akimasuka

7 chiketto o yonmai onegai shimasu

## 3 Translation

1 *(Please) turn left.*

2 *Is there a museum in town?*

3 *Fill it up, please.*

4 *Where are we?*

5 *There's a swimming pool near the bridge.*

6 *What time do you open?*

7 *I'd like four tickets.*

**2** headlight

**3** bumper

## 4 Directions

Ask how to get to these places:

1 *temple*

2 *station*

3 *internet café*

4 *cinema*

## 4 Directions

1 寺にはどうやって行
けばいいですか？
tera niwa dohyatte
ikeba iidesuka

2 駅にはどうやって
行けばいいです
か？
eki niwa dohyatte
ikeba iidesuka

3 ネットカフェには
どうやって行けば
いいですか？
netto kafeh niwa
dohyatte ikeba
iidesuka

4 映画館にはどうや
って行けばいいで
すか？
eiga kan niwa
dohyatte ikeba
iidesuka

## 1 Warm up

Ask "How much is that?" (pp.18–19)

What are "breakfast", "lunch", and "dinner"? (pp.20–21)

What are "three", "four", "five", and "six"? (pp.10–11)

# Heya no yoyaku
*Booking a room*

Japan has a large number of international hotels as well as the traditional Japanese inns (see pp.62–3). **Rabuhoteru** (*love hotels*) rentable by the hour are best avoided. The famous tubular **kapuseruhoteru** (*capsule hotels*) are also available in major cities, but aren't suitable for the claustrophobic.

## 2 Useful phrases

Practise these phrases and then test yourself by concealing the Japanese on the left with the cover flap.

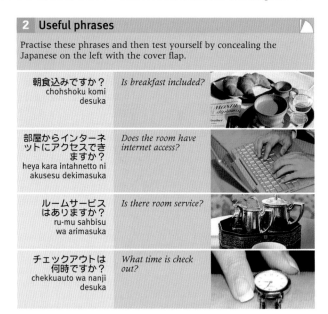

| | |
|---|---|
| 朝食込みですか？<br>chohshoku komi desuka | *Is breakfast included?* |
| 部屋からインターネットにアクセスできますか？<br>heya kara intahnetto ni akusesu dekimasuka | *Does the room have internet access?* |
| ルームサービスはありますか？<br>ru-mu sahbisu wa arimasuka | *Is there room service?* |
| チェックアウトは何時ですか？<br>chekkuauto wa nanji desuka | *What time is check out?* |

## 3 In conversation

空いている部屋はありますか？
aiteiru heya wa arimasuka

*Do you have any rooms?*

はい。ダブルルームがございます。
hai. daburu ru-mu ga gozaimasu

*Yes, we have a double room.*

ルームサービスはありますか？
ru-mu sahbisu wa arimasuka

*Is there room service?*

### 4 Words to remember

Familiarize yourself with these words and test yourself by concealing the Japanese on the right with the cover flap.

部屋から海が見えま
すか？
heya kara umi ga mie
masuka
*Does the room have
a sea view?*

### 5 Say it

Do you have any
single rooms?

For two nights.

Is dinner included?

| | | |
|---|---|---|
| room | 部屋 | heya |
| single room | シングルルーム | shinguru ru-mu |
| double room | ダブルルーム | daburu ru-mu |
| twin room | ツインルーム | tsuin ru-mu |
| bathroom | バス | basu |
| shower | シャワー | shawah |
| breakfast | 朝食 | chohshoku |
| key | キー | kih |
| balcony | バルコニー | barukonih |
| two nights | 二泊 | ni haku |
| three nights | 三泊 | san paku |

---

◉ **Cultural tip** Japanese hotel rooms tend to include a pair of house slippers as a matter of course. You are assumed to want to remove your shoes in the room, as you would at home. Hotel staff address customers using ultra-polite, uncommon Japanese expressions.

はい。何泊のご予定
ですか？
hai. nan paku no
goyoteh desuka

*Yes. How many
nights?*

三泊です。
san paku desu

*For three nights.*

かしこまりました。
これがキーです。
kashikomari mashita.
kore ga kih desu

*Very good. Here's your
key.*

How do you say "Is/Are there...?", "There is/are...", and "There isn't/aren't...?" (pp.48–9)

What's the Japanese for "room"? (pp.58–59)

# Hoteru de
## *In the hotel*

As well as slippers, you will nearly always find a traditional Japanese robe/pyjamas (**yukata**) in your room – usually laid out on the bed. This is the case even in the international chains. Non-smoking rooms are sometimes offered, but exclusively non-smoking floors are not always available.

## **2** Match and repeat

Match the numbered items in this hotel bedroom with the Japanese text in the panel and test yourself using the cover flap.

1 ベッドサイド
テーブル
beddo saido
tehburu

2 ランプ
ranpu

3 カーテン
kahten

4 ソファ
sofa

5 枕
makura

6 ベッド
beddo

7 ベッドスプレッド
beddo supureddo

8 毛布
mohfu

- **1** bedside table
- **2** lamp
- **3** curtains
- sofa **4**
- **5** pillow
- **6** bed
- **7** bedspread
- blanket **8**

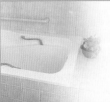

🔲 **Cultural tip** Japanese bathrooms can be a culture shock to visitors. The bathtubs are smaller as they are generally only used for soaping yourself before rinsing under the shower. The toilets often feature hi-tech gadgets, such as heated seats. Some even act as automatic bidets, with an in-built washer and drier.

## 3  Useful phrases

Learn these phrases and then test yourself using the cover flap.

| | | |
|---|---|---|
| | *The room is too hot.* | 部屋が暑すぎます。<br>heya ga atsu sugi masu |
| | *The room is too cold.* | 部屋が寒すぎます。<br>heya ga samu sugi masu |
| | *There aren't any towels.* | タオルがありません。<br>taoru ga arimasen |
| | *I'd like some soap.* | 石けんを下さい。<br>sekken o kudasai |
| | *The shower seems to be broken.* | シャワーが壊れているようです。<br>shawah ga kowarete iruyoh desu |

## 4  Put into practice

Cover the text on the right and then complete the dialogue in Japanese.

| | | |
|---|---|---|
| | はい、フロントでございます。<br>hai, furonto de gozaimasu<br>*Yes, front desk.* | 枕はありますか？<br>makura wa arimasuka |
| | *Say: Are there any pillows?* | |
| | 部屋の担当者が持って参ります。<br>heya no tantoh-sha ga motte mairimasu<br>*The staff will bring you some.* | それからテレビが壊れているようです。<br>sorekara terebi ga kowarete iruyoh desu |
| | *Say: And the television seems to be broken.* | |

# Ryokan to onsen
## *Inns and spas*

Traditional Japanese inns, **ryokan**, and spas with hot springs, **onsen**, are often based in beautiful surroundings and offer a haven of peace. Prices are usually inclusive of accommodation and all meals. Additional health treatments such as massage are often also available.

### 1 Warm up

What is Japanese for "shower" (pp.60–1), and "swimming pool"? (pp.48–9)

Say "I'd like some towels". (pp.60–1)

### 2 Match and repeat

Learn these phrases and then test yourself by concealing the Japanese with the cover flap.

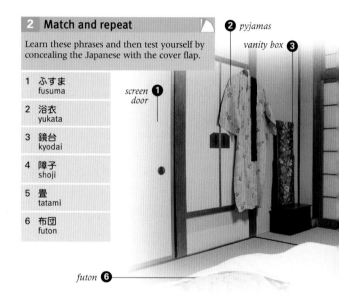

② *pyjamas*

*vanity box* ③

*screen door* ①

*futon* ⑥

1 ふすま
fusuma

2 浴衣
yukata

3 鏡台
kyodai

4 障子
shoji

5 畳
tatami

6 布団
futon

### 3 In conversation

二泊したいのですが。
ni haku shitai no desuga

*I'd like to stay for two nights.*

かしこまりました。
kashikomari mashita

*Certainly.*

この旅館に温泉はありますか？
kono ryokan ni onsen wa arimasuka

*Is there a hot spring (tub) in the inn?*

## 5 Say it

I'd like to stay for five nights.

Is there a swimming pool in the inn?

Can I rent "yukata" pyjamas?

**4** *screen window*

**5** *tatami mat*

## 4 Useful phrases

Learn these phrases. Read the English under the pictures and say the phrase in Japanese as shown on the right. Then cover up the answers on the right and test yourself.

*What type of hot springs do you have?*

どんなタイプの温泉
ですか？
donna taipu no onsen
desuka

*Is there a sauna?*

サウナはあります
か？
sauna wa arimasuka

*Can I book a massage?*

マッサージを予約で
きますか？
massahji o yoyaku
dekimasuka

*Can I rent a towel?*

タオルを借りることが
できますか？
taoru o karirukoto ga
dekimasuka

はい。屋上にござい
ます。
hai. okujoh ni
gozaimasu

*Yes, it's located on the roof.*

タオルを借りることが
できますか？
taoru o karirukoto ga
dekimasuka

*Can I rent a towel?*

入り口で貸し出して
おります。
iriguchi de kashidashite
orimasu

*You can rent one at the spa entrance.*

## 1 Warm up

How do you say
"My son has a car"?
(pp.14–15)

What is the Japanese
for "room", "bed",
and "pillow"?
(pp.60–1)

# Keiyoh-shi
## *Adjectives*

Basic adjectives (descriptive words)
are quite simple to use in Japanese:
*car(s)* is **kuruma**; *small car(s)* is **chihsai
kuruma**. In a sentence, the word order
is: *item(s)* + **wa/ga** *("as for")* + *adjective*
+ **desu**, for example **kuruma wa chihsai
desu** *("The car is small")*; **yama wa takai
desu** *("The mountains are high")*.

## 2 Words to remember

There are no plurals in Japanese. So "the mountain is high" and
"the mountains are high" would both be **yama wa takai desu**.

| 大きい ohkih | *big, large* |
|---|---|
| 小さい chihsai | *small* |
| 高い takai | *high, tall* |
| 低い hikui | *short* |
| 暑い atsui | *hot* |
| 冷たい tsumetai | *cold* |
| 静か shizuka | *quiet* |
| うるさい urusai | *noisy* |
| 硬い katai | *hard* |
| 柔らかい yawarakai | *soft* |
| 美しい utsukushih | *beautiful* |

山は高いです。
yama wa takai desu
*The mountains are high.*

森が綺麗です。
mori ga kireh desu
*The forest is
beautiful.*

**● Read it** All of the adjectives above
except "noisy" are written in a mixture of
kanji and hiragana characters. The first kanji
character carries the core meaning, for
example 大 ("big"), 美 ("beautiful").
The attached hiragana characters are
grammatical endings. Look up the hiragana
characters in the table on pp. 158–9 to
identify the syllables they represent.

寺は古いです。
tera wa furui desu
*The temple is old.*

あの橋はとても狭いです。
ano hashi wa totemo semai
desu
*That bridge is very narrow*

## 3 Useful phrases

You can emphasize a description by using **totemo** (*very*) before the adjective: **totemo urusai** (*very noisy*).

| | | |
|---|---|---|
| | *The coffee is cold.* | コーヒーが冷たいです。<br>koh-hi ga tsumetai desu |
| | *My room is very noisy.* | 私の部屋はとてもうるさいです。<br>watashi no heya wa totemo urusai desu |
| | *This car is very small.* | この車はとても小さいです。<br>kono kuruma wa totemo chihsai desu |
| | *This bed is hard.* | このベッドは硬いです。<br>kono beddo wa katai desu |

## 4 Put into practice

Join in this conversation. Cover up the text on the right and complete the dialogue in Japanese. Check and repeat if necessary.

| | | |
|---|---|---|
| | こちらが部屋です。<br>kochira ga heya desu<br>*Here's the room.*<br><br>*Say: The view is very beautiful.* | 景色がとても美しいです。<br>keshiki ga totemo utsukushih desu |
| | バスルームはあちらです。<br>basu ru-mu wa achira desu<br>*The bathroom is over there.*<br><br>*Say: It's very small.* | とても小さいです。<br>totemo chihsai desu |
| | あいにく他には部屋はございません。<br>ainiku hoka niwa heya wa gozaimasen<br>*Unfortunately, there aren't any other rooms.*<br><br>*Say: We'll take it.* | これにします。<br>kore ni shimasu |

# Fukushu to kurikaeshi
*Review and repeat*

**Kotae**
*Answers*
Cover with flap

## 1 Adjectives

## 1 Adjectives

1 大きい
ohkih

2 柔らかい
yawarakai

3 古い
furui

4 静か
shizuka

5 冷たい
tsumetai

Put the word in brackets into Japanese.

1 ie wa _____ **(big)** desu

2 beddo wa _____ **(soft)** desu

3 tera wa totemo _____ **(old)** desu

4 watashi no heya wa _____ **(quiet)** desu

5 mizu ga totemo _____ **(cold)** desu

## 2 Inns

## 2 Inns

1 ふすま
fusuma

2 浴衣
yukata

3 鏡台
kyodai

4 布団
futon

5 障子
shoji

6 畳
tatami

Name these items you might find
in a traditional Japanese inn.

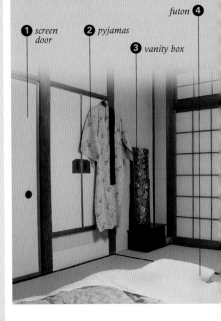

*futon* 4

1 *screen door*

2 *pyjamas*

3 *vanity box*

**Kotae**
*Answers*
Cover with flap

## 3 At the hotel

You are booking a room in a hotel. Follow the conversation, replying in Japanese using the English prompts.

hai, dohzo
1 *Do you have any rooms?*

hai. nanpaku no goyoteh desuka
2 *Five nights.*

kashikomari mashita
3 *Is breakfast included?*

ihe. go-hyaku yen desu
4 *We'll take it.*

### 3 At the hotel

1 空いている部屋はありますか？
aiteiru heya wa arimasuka

2 五泊です。
go haku desu

3 朝食込みですか？
chohshoku komi desuka

4 これにします。
kore ni shimasu

---

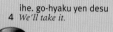

**⑤** *screen window*

*tatami mat* **⑥**

## 4 Negatives

Make these sentences negative using **wa arimasen**.

1 taoru wa arimasu

2 ru-mu sahbisu wa arimasu

3 kono ryokan ni onsen wa arimasu

4 kono machi ni hakubutsu kan wa arimasu

5 meishi wa arimasu

### 4 Negatives

1 タオルはありません。
taoru wa arimasen

2 ルームサービスはありません。
ru-mu sahbisu wa arimasen

3 この旅館に温泉はありません。
kono ryokan ni onsen wa arimasen

4 この街に博物館はありません。
kono machi ni hakubutsu kan wa arimasen

5 名刺はありません。
meishi wa arimasen

Ask "Can I use a credit card?" (p.39)

Say "Turn left at the traffic lights", and "The station is near the café". (pp.50–1)

# Depahto
## *Department store*

In recent years, many Japanese have started buying food and other provisions in **depahto**. The basement floor of department stores usually houses a food "market" with separate stalls. However, many towns also have shopping arcades, often adjacent to local train stations.

## 2   Match and repeat

Notice the Japanese word **ya**, meaning *shop*: **pan ya,** *bread shop (baker)*; **niku ya,** *meat shop (butcher)*, etc. Match the shops numbered 1–9 below and right to the Japanese in the panel.

1  パン屋
   pan ya

2  ケーキ屋
   kehki ya

3  酒屋
   saka ya

4  デリカテッセン
   derikatessen

5  八百屋
   yao ya

6  本屋
   hon ya

7  魚屋
   sakana ya

8  肉屋
   niku ya

9  豆腐屋
   tofu ya

❶ *baker*

❷ *cake shop*

❹ *delicatessen*

❺ *greengrocer*

❼ *fishmonger*

❽ *butcher*

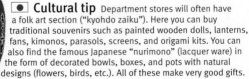

🔲 **Cultural tip** Department stores will often have a folk art section ("kyohdo zaiku"). Here you can buy traditional souvenirs such as painted wooden dolls, lanterns, fans, kimonos, parasols, screens, and origami kits. You can also find the famous Japanese "nurimono" (lacquer ware) in the form of decorated bowls, boxes, and pots with natural designs (flowers, birds, etc.). All of these make very good gifts.

## 3  Words to remember

Familiarize yourself with these words and then test yourself.

花屋はどこですか？
hana ya wa doko
desuka
*Where's the florist?*

| | | |
|---|---|---|
| *dairy* | 乳製品 | nyu seihin |
| *antique shop* | 骨董品店 | kotto hin ten |
| *hairdresser* | 美容院 | biyoh in |
| *barber* | 理容院 | riyoh in |
| *jeweller* | 宝石商 | hohseki shoh |
| *post office* | 郵便局 | yu-bin kyoku |
| *florist* | 花屋 | hana ya |
| *shoe shop* | 靴屋 | kutsu ya |
| *travel agent* | 旅行代理店 | ryokoh dairi den |

❸ *off-licence*

❻ *bookshop*

❾ *tofu shop*

## 4  Useful phrases

Familiarize yourself with these phrases.

| | |
|---|---|
| *Where's the hairdresser?* | 美容院はどこですか？ biyoh in wa doko desuka |
| *Where can I pay?* | どこで払えますか？ doko de harae masuka |
| *I'm just looking. Thanks.* | 見ているだけです。どうも。 mite iru dake desu. dohmo |
| *Do you have phonecards?* ("Are there phonecards?") | テレカはあります か？ tereka wa arimasuka |
| *Can I exchange this?* | 交換できますか？ kohkan dekimasuka |
| *Can you give me the receipt?* | レシートをもらえ ますか？ reshihto o morae masuka |
| *I'd like to place an order for…* | …を注文したい です。 …o chu-mon shitai desu |

## 5  Say it

Where's the baker?

Do you have towels?

I'd like to place an order for curtains.

### 1 Warm up

What are "forty", "seventy", "a hundred", "a thousand", and "ten thousand" in Japanese? (pp. 30–1)

Say "big" and "small" in Japanese. (pp.64–5)

# Denkiya
## *Electronics store*

Tokyo is home to probably the world's largest concentration of electronics stores in the famous Akihabara "electric town". Here you can find a huge range of computers, cameras, gadgets, and parts, both new and second-hand. Guarantees vary, and you need to check the equipment will work at home.

## 2 Match and repeat

Match the numbered items to the Japanese words in the panel on the left and test yourself using the cover flap.

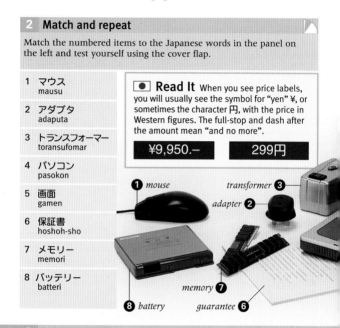

1 マウス
   mausu

2 アダプタ
   adaputa

3 トランスフォーマー
   toransufomar

4 パソコン
   pasokon

5 画面
   gamen

6 保証書
   hoshoh-sho

7 メモリー
   memori

8 バッテリー
   batteri

> **Read It** When you see price labels, you will usually see the symbol for "yen" ¥, or sometimes the character 円, with the price in Western figures. The full-stop and dash after the amount mean "and no more".
>
> ¥9,950.–      299円

❶ mouse
transformer ❸
adapter ❷
memory ❼
❽ battery
guarantee ❻

## 3 In conversation

あのパソコンは
いくらですか？
ano pasokon wa ikura
desuka

*How much is that laptop computer?*

税込み10万円です。
zeikomi jyu-man yen
desu

*It's 100,000 yen including tax.*

ハードディスクの
容量はいくらですか？
hardo disuku no yoryo wa
ikura desuka

*How big is the hard disk?*

◉ **Cultural tip** The Japanese currency system is the yen (¥). As each yen is worth less then 1p, you'll generally be spending thousands, or even tens of thousands of them. Banknote denominations go up to ¥10,000, so be careful not to confuse the number of zeros.

④ *laptop*

⑤ *screen*

### 4 Useful phrases

Learn these phrases. Then conceal the answers on the right using the cover flap. Read the English under the pictures and say the phrase in Japanese as shown on the right.

あのカメラは
高すぎます。
ano kamera wa
takasugi masu

*That camera is too expensive.*

あれはいくら
ですか?
a-re wa ikura desuka

*How much is that one?*

イギリスで使
えますか?
igirisu de tsukae
masuka

*Will it work in England?*

40ギガで、メモリー
は1ギガです。
yonjyu giga de memori
wa ichi giga desu

*40 gigabytes, and one gigabyte of memory.*

イギリスで使え
ますか?
igirisu de tsukae masuka

*Will it work in England?*

はい。ただしトランスフ
オーマーが必要です。
hai. tadashi toransufomar
ga hitsuyo desu

*Yes, but you need a transformer.*

What are these items, which you could buy in a supermarket? (pp.22–3)

yasai
kudamono
shifudo
kome
wain
mizu

# Su-pah de
## *At the supermarket*

Japanese supermarkets are often more like hypermarkets, selling household items and clothes as well as food and essentials. Most Japanese still pay for their groceries in cash. Paying by card at a supermarket is still not common, but cards are frequently used in other stores, such as clothing stores.

**2** Match and repeat

Look at the numbered items and match them to the Japanese words in the panel on the left.

1 家庭用品
kateh yo-hin

2 果物
kudamono

3 飲み物
nomimono

4 加工食品
kakoh shokuhin

5 野菜
yasai

6 冷凍食品
reitoh shokuhin

7 菓子類
kashi rui

8 化粧品
keshoh hin

household products ❶

*fruit* ❷

*drinks* ❸

*ready meals* ❹

*vegetables* ❺

*frozen foods* ❻

● **Cultural tip** Supermarkets usually pre-package fresh produce such as meat, fish, fruit, vegetables, and cheese. You just pick up the pre-priced packet you want and take it to the checkout.

## 3 Useful phrases

Learn these phrases and then test yourself using the cover flap.

| | |
|---|---|
| *May I have a bag, please?* | ビニール袋をもらえますか？<br>binihru bukuro o moraemsuka |
| *Where's the drinks section?* | 飲み物類はどこですか？<br>nomimono rui wa doko desuka |
| *Where's the checkout?* | レジはどこですか？<br>reji wa doko desuka |
| *Where are the shopping trolleys?* | ショッピングカートはどこですか？<br>shoppingu kahto wa doko desuka |

## 4 Words to remember

Learn these words and then test yourself using the cover flap.

**8** beauty products

**7** snacks

| | |
|---|---|
| *bread* | パン<br>pan |
| *milk* | 牛乳<br>gyu-nyu |
| *butter* | バター<br>batah |
| *dairy products* | 乳製品<br>nyu seihin |
| *ham* | ハム<br>hamu |
| *salt* | 塩<br>shio |
| *pepper* | 胡椒<br>koshoh |
| *toilet paper* | トイレットペーパー<br>toiretto pehpah |
| *nappies* | オムツ<br>omutsu |
| *washing-up liquid* | 食器用洗剤<br>shokki yoh senzai |

## 5 Say it

Where's the toilet paper?

May I have some butter, please?

Is there any ham?

## 1 Warm up

Say "A..., please".
(pp.24–5)

Ask "Is there a...?"
(pp.48–9)

Say "thirteen",
"twenty-four", and
"thirty". (pp.30–1)

Say "big" and
"small". (pp.64–5)

# Fuku to kutsu
## Clothes and shoes

Loan words are used for most Western-style clothes: **pantsu** (*trousers*), **jyaketto** (*jacket*), etc. Only items that existed traditionally have Japanese names: **kutsu** (*shoes*), **sode** (*sleeves*). Other traditional articles, such as the **kimono**, **obi** (*sash*), and **geta** (*clogs*) are now largely reserved for special occasions.

## 2 Match and repeat

Match the numbered items of clothing to the Japanese words in the panel on the left. Test yourself using the cover flap.

1 シャツ
  shatsu

2 ネクタイ
  nekutai

3 袖
  sode

4 ジャケット
  jyaketto

5 ポケット
  poketto

6 パンツ
  pantsu

7 スカート
  sukahto

8 ストッキング
  sutokkingu

9 靴
  kutsu

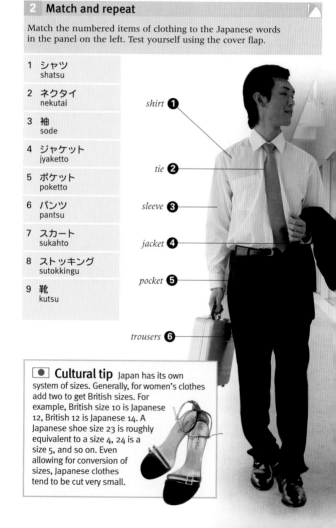

*shirt* **1**

*tie* **2**

*sleeve* **3**

*jacket* **4**

*pocket* **5**

*trousers* **6**

**● Cultural tip** Japan has its own system of sizes. Generally, for women's clothes add two to get British sizes. For example, British size 10 is Japanese 12, British 12 is Japanese 14. A Japanese shoe size 23 is roughly equivalent to a size 4, 24 is a size 5, and so on. Even allowing for conversion of sizes, Japanese clothes tend to be cut very small.

## 3 Useful phrases

Learn these phrases and then test yourself using the cover flap.

| | |
|---|---|
| *Do you have a larger size?* | もっと大きいサイズがありますか？<br>motto ohkih saizu ga arimasuka |
| *It's not what I want.* | わたしが欲しいものではありません。<br>watashi ga hoshih mono dewa arimasen |
| *I'll take the pink one.* | ピンクのを買います。<br>pinku no o kaimasu |

## 4 Words to remember

Colours are adjectives (see p.64). Below you will see the pure form of the colours, but you may find that endings have been added to the word depending on the sentence.

| | | |
|---|---|---|
| *red* | 赤 | aka |
| *white* | 白 | shiro |
| *blue* | 青 | ao |
| *yellow* | 黄色 | ki iro |
| *green* | 緑 | midori |
| *black* | 黒 | kuro |

**7** *skirt*

**8** *tights*

**9** *shoes*

● **Read it** All the items of clothing in section 2, except "shoes" and "sleeve", are written in kata-kana, the script used for foreign loan words. Use the katakana table on pp. 158–9 to work out the syllables in each word.

**Kotae**
*Answers*
Cover with flap

# Fukushu to kurikaeshi
## *Review and repeat*

### 1 Electronic

1 マウス
  mausu

2 アダプタ
  adaputa

3 トランスフォー
  マー
  toransufomar

4 画面
  gamen

5 バッテリー
  batteri

6 メモリー
  memori

7 保証書
  hoshoh-sho

8 パソコン
  pasokon

### 1 Electronic

Name the numbered items in Japanese.

**1** mouse
**2** adapter
**3** transformer
**4** screen
**5** battery
**6** memory
**7** guarantee
**8** laptop

### 2 Description

1 *That camera is too expensive.*

2 *My room is very noisy.*

3 *Do you have a larger size?*

### 2 Description

What do these phrases mean?

1 ano kamera wa takasugi masu

2 watashi no heya wa totemo urusai desu

3 motto ohkih saizu ga arimasuka

### 3 Shops

1 パン屋
  pan ya

2 デリカテッセン
  derikatessen

3 八百屋
  yao ya

4 魚屋
  sakana ya

5 ケーキ屋
  kehki ya

6 肉屋
  niku ya

### 3 Shops

Name the numbered shops in Japanese.
Then check your answers.

**1** baker
**2** delicatessen
**3** greengrocer
**4** fishmonger
**5** cake shop
**6** butcher

## Kotae
*Answers*
**Cover with flap**

### 4 Supermarket

What is the Japanese for the numbered product categories?

❶ *household products*

❷ *beauty products*

❸ *drinks*

❹ *snacks*

❺ *frozen foods*

### 4 Supermarket

1 家庭用品
  kateh yo-hin

2 化粧品
  keshoh hin

3 飲み物
  nomimono

4 菓子類
  kashi rui

5 冷凍食品
  reitoh shokuhin

### 5 Museum

Join in this conversation replying in Japanese following the English prompts.

hai, dohzo
1 *I'd like four tickets.*

happyaku yen ni narimasu
2 *What time do you close?*

roku ji ni shimari masu
3 *Is there a guidebook?*

dohzo. gaido bukku wa muryoh desu
4 *Where's the lift?*

achira ni erebehtah ga arimasu
5 *Thank you very much.*

### 5 Museum

1 チケットを四枚
  お願いします。
  chiketto o yonmai
  onegai shimasu

2 何時に閉まり
  ますか？
  nanji ni
  shimarimasuka

3 ガイドブック
  はありますか？
  gaido bukku wa
  arimasuka

4 エレベーターはど
  こですか？
  erebehtah wa
  doko desuka

5 どうもありがと
  うございます。
  dohmo arigatoh
  gozaimasu

## 1 Warm up

Say "Akiko is a student" and "I'm English". (pp.14–15)

Say "The internet café is in the centre of town". (pp.48–9)

# Shigoto
*Jobs*

Japanese has some generic, non-job specific words used to refer mainly to office workers: the self-explanatory **sararihman** (*salary man*) and the **OL** (pronounced *"oh-el"* and meaning *"office lady"*) being two of the most common. **Sengyo-shufu** (literally *"specialist"*) is used to mean *housewife*.

## 2 Words to remember: jobs

Familiarize yourself with these Japanese words and test yourself using the flap.

| | |
|---|---|
| 医者 isha | *doctor* |
| 歯医者 ha-isha | *dentist* |
| 看護師 kangoshi | *nurse* |
| 先生 sensei | *teacher* |
| 会計士 kaikehshi | *accountant* |
| 弁護士 bengoshi | *lawyer* |
| デザイナー dezainah | *designer* |
| 秘書 hisho | *secretary* |
| 店主 tenshu | *shopkeeper* |
| 電気技師 denki gishi | *electrician* |
| 配管工 haikankoh | *plumber* |
| コック kokku | *cook* |
| 自営業 ji-eigyoh | *self-employed* |
| 学生 gakusei | *student* |

会社員です。
kaisha in desu
*I'm a businessman.*

会計士です。
kaikehshi desu
*I'm an accountant.*

## 3 Put into practice

Join in this conversation. Use the cover flap to conceal the text on the right and complete the dialogue in Japanese.

| | |
|---|---|
| ご職業は？<br>goshokugyoh wa<br>*What's your profession?*<br><br>*Say: I'm an accountant.* | 会計士です。<br>kaikehshi desu |
| どこの会社にお勤めですか？<br>doko no kaisha ni otsutomete desuka<br>*What company do you work for?*<br><br>*Say: I'm self-employed.* | 自営業です。<br>ji-eigyoh desu |
| ああ、そうなんですか！<br>ah, sohnandesuka<br>*Oh, really!*<br><br>*Ask: What's your profession?* | ご職業は？<br>goshokugyoh wa |

🔘 **Cultural tip** There are different titles for "manager" depending on the level. The order of seniority is 社長 **shacho** (MD), 専務 **senmu** (division), 部長 **bucho** (department), 課長 **kacho** (section), 係長 **kakaricho** (team). Look out for the titles on business cards.

## 4 Words to remember: workplace

Familiarize yourself with these words and test yourself.

| | |
|---|---|
| *head office* | 本社<br>honsha |
| *branch* | 支店<br>shiten |
| *...department* | ...部<br>...bu |
| *office worker* | 会社員<br>kaisha in |
| *manager* | マネージャー<br>manehjyah |

本社は大阪にあります。
honsha wa Osaka ni arimasu
*The head office is in Osaka.*

**1 Warm up**

Practise different ways of introducing yourself in different situations (pp.8–9). Mention your name, occupation, and any other information you'd like to volunteer (pp.12–13, pp.14–15).

# Ofisu
## *The office*

Traditionally most adult Japanese would have an **inkan**, an official seal or stamp unique to the individual and used to sign papers and forms. You may still see these stamps on official government papers and high-level contracts, although they are no longer the necessity they once were.

## 2 Words to remember

Familiarize yourself with these words. Read them aloud several times and try to memorize them. Conceal the Japanese with the cover flap and test yourself.

| | |
|---|---|
| コンピュータ<br>konpyu-tah | computer |
| マウス<br>mausu | mouse |
| メール<br>mehru | e-mail |
| インターネット<br>intahnetto | internet |
| パスワード<br>pasuwahdo | password |
| ボイスメール<br>boisu mehru | voicemail |
| ファックス<br>fakkusu | fax machine |
| コピー<br>kopih | photocopy |
| コピー機<br>kopihki | photocopier<br>("copy machine") |
| 本<br>hon | book |
| 手帳<br>techoh | diary |
| 名刺<br>meishi | business card |
| ミーティング<br>mihtingu | meeting |
| コンフェレンス<br>konferensu | conference |
| 会議事項<br>kaigi jikoh | agenda |

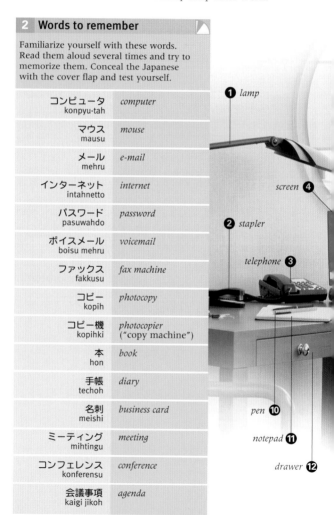

❶ lamp

screen ❹

❷ stapler

telephone ❸

pen ❿

notepad ⓫

drawer ⓬

## 3 Useful phrases

Learn these phrases and then test yourself using the cover flap.

| | | |
|---|---|---|
| | *I need to make some photocopies.* | コピーをとる必要が あります。<br>kopih o toru hitsuyoh ga arimasu |
| | *I'd like to arrange an appointment.* | アポを取りたいの ですが。<br>apo o toritai no desuga |
| | *I want to send an e-mail.* | メールを送りたい です。<br>mehru o okuritai desu |

## 4 Match and repeat

Match the numbered items to the Japanese words on the right.

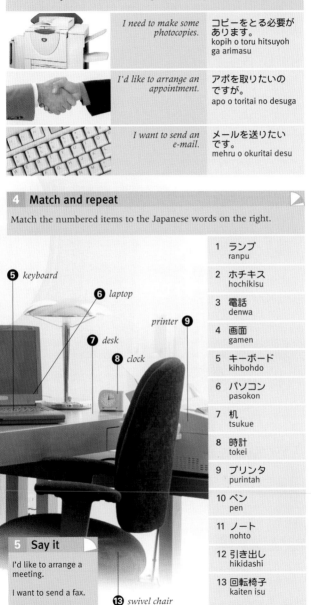

**5** *keyboard*

**6** *laptop*

*printer* **9**

**7** *desk*

**8** *clock*

**13** *swivel chair*

1 ランプ
ranpu

2 ホチキス
hochikisu

3 電話
denwa

4 画面
gamen

5 キーボード
kihbohdo

6 パソコン
pasokon

7 机
tsukue

8 時計
tokei

9 プリンタ
purintah

10 ペン
pen

11 ノート
nohto

12 引き出し
hikidashi

13 回転椅子
kaiten isu

## 5 Say it

I'd like to arrange a meeting.

I want to send a fax.

Is there an agenda?

## 1 Warm up

Say "Oh, really?!"
(pp.78–9), "meeting"
(pp.80–1), and
"appointment".
(pp.32–3)

Ask "What's your
profession?" and
answer "I'm a lawyer".
(pp.78–9)

# Gakkai de
## *At the conference*

University courses usually last four
years and entrance to the top colleges
is very competitive. High schools often
start to prepare for the entrance exam
many years in advance as future
prospects can depend on which
university a student attends. Once
there, the pressure is less intense.

## 2 Useful phrases

Learn these phrases and then test yourself using the cover flap.

| ご専門は？ gosenmon wa | *What's your field?* |
| 研究をしています。 kenkyu o shiteimasu | *I'm doing research.* |
| 法律を勉強しました。 hohritsu o benkyoh shimashita | *I have a degree in law.* |
| 建築学の講師です。 kenchiku gaku no kohshi desu | *I'm a lecturer in architecture.* |

## 3 In conversation

こんにちは。岡田
です。
konnichiwa. Okada desu

*Hello, I'm Okada.*

どこで教えていらっ
しゃいますか？
doko de oshiete irasshai
masuka

*Where do you teach?*

東京大学です。
Tokyo daigaku desu

*I teach at Tokyo University.*

## 4 Words to remember

Familiarize yourself with these words and then test yourself.

展示会には私達のスタ
ンドがあります。
tenji kai niwa watashitachi
no sutando ga arimasu
*There's our exhibition
stand.*

| | | |
|---|---|---|
| *conference (academic)* | 学会 | gakkai |
| *lecture* | 講義 | kohgi |
| *seminar* | ゼミ | zemi |
| *lecture theatre* | 講堂 | kohdoh |
| *exhibition* | 展示会 | tenji kai |
| *university lecturer* | 大学講師 | daigaku kohshi |
| *professor* | 教授 | kyohjyu |
| *medicine* | 医学 | igaku |
| *science* | 科学 | kagaku |
| *literature* | 文学 | bungaku |
| *engineering* | 工学 | kohgaku |
| *law* | 法律 | hohritsu |
| *architecture* | 建築学 | kenchiku gaku |
| *information technology* | IT | "ai-tih" |

## 5 Say it

I teach at London University.

I have a degree in medicine.

I'm a lecturer in engineering.

ご専門は？
gosenmon wa

*What's your field?*

物理です。研究もし
ています。
butsuri desu. kenkyu
mo shiteimasu

*Physics. I'm also doing
research.*

ああ、そうですか。
ah, sohdesuka

*Oh, really?*

Say "I want to send an e-mail". (pp.80–1)

Say "I'd like to arrange an appointment". (pp.80–1)

# Bijinesu
## *In business*

You will make a good impression if you make the effort to begin a meeting with a few words in Japanese, even if your vocabulary is limited. After that, all parties will probably be happy to continue in English. Remember to take business cards to exchange at meetings.

**2** Words to remember

Familiarize yourself with these words and then test yourself by concealing the Japanese with the cover flap.

| | |
|---|---|
| 注文<br>chu-mon | *order* |
| 配達<br>haitatsu | *delivery* |
| 支払い<br>shiharai | *payment* |
| 予算<br>yosan | *budget* |
| 値段<br>nedan | *price* |
| 証書<br>shohsho | *documents* |
| 請求書<br>sehkyu-sho | *invoice* |
| 見積もり<br>mitsumori | *estimate* |
| 利益<br>ri-eki | *profits* |
| 売り上げ<br>uri age | *sales* |
| 合計額<br>gohkeh gaku | *figures* |

顧客<br>kokyaku<br>*client*

報告書<br>hohkoku sho<br>*report*

🔳 **Cultural tip** In general, business dealings are formal. However, the Japanese are famous for their hospitality. Visitors are often escorted from the moment they wake up to the moment they go to bed. It's a good idea to take presents from home to show your appreciation.

## 3 Useful phrases

Practise these phrases. Notice that the Japanese is necessarily very polite. It's better to err on the side of caution in a business context.

契約書を見せて
ください。
kehyaku sho o misete
kudasai
*Please show me the
contract.*

重役
jyu-yaku
*executive*

契約書を送ってくだ
さいますか？
kehyaku sho o okutte
kudasai masuka

*Can you send me the
contract, please?*

値段は決まりました
か？
nedan wa
kimarimashitaka

*Have we agreed a
price?*

配達はいつになりま
すか？
haitatsu wa itsu ni nari
masuka

*When can you make
the delivery?*

予算はおいくら
ですか？
yosan wa oikura
desuka

*What's the budget?*

### 4 Say it

Can you send me the
invoice, please?

What's the price?

Please show me the
order.

---

● **Read it** Some traditional Japanese
words used in a business context have
alternative English loan words. These
imported words will be written in katakana
characters. For example, you may see the
following alternatives for the traditional
words in this lesson. See if you can work out
the individual syllables of the words using
the katakana table on pp.158-9.

オーダー **ohdah** *order*

ドキュメント **dokyumento** *document*

レポート **repohto** *report*

## Kotae
*Answers*
Cover with flap

# Fukushu to kurikaeshi
*Review and repeat*

**1 At the office**

1 ランプ
  ranpu

2 パソコン
  pasokon

3 ペン
  pen

4 ホチキス
  hochikisu

5 机
  tsukue

6 ノート
  nohto

7 時計
  tokei

### 1 At the office

Name these items in Japanese.

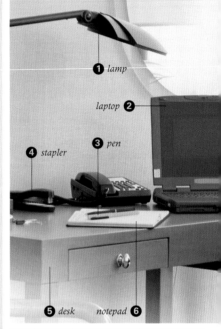

**1** *lamp*

*laptop* **2**

**3** *pen*

**4** *stapler*

**5** *desk*    *notepad* **6**

### 2 Jobs

1 医者
  isha

2 配管工
  haikankoh

3 店主
  tenshu

4 会計士
  kaikehshi

5 学生
  gakusei

6 弁護士
  bengoshi

### 2 Jobs

What are these jobs in Japanese?

1 *doctor*

2 *plumber*

3 *shopkeeper*

4 *accountant*

5 *student*

6 *lawyer*

## 3 Work

Answer these questions following the English prompts.

goshokugyoh wa
1 *Say "I'm a dentist".*

doko no kaisha ni otsutome desuka
2 *Say "I'm self-employed".*

doko de oshiete irasshai masuka
3 *Say "I teach at Tokyo university".*

moshi moshi
4 *Say "I'd like to arrange an appointment".*

clock **7**

## 3 Work

1 歯医者です。
ha-isha desu

2 自営業です。
ji-eigyoh desu

3 東京大学です。
Tokyo daigaku desu

4 アポを取りたいのですが。
apo o toritai no desuga

## 4 How much?

Answer the question with the price shown in brackets.

1 koh-hi wa ikura desuka
(¥300)

2 heya wa ikura desuka
(¥8,000)

3 pasokon wa ikura desuka
(¥100,000)

4 chiketto wa ikura desuka
(¥700)

## 4 How much?

1 三百円です。
san byaku yen desu

2 八千円です。
hassen yen desu

3 十万円です。
jyu-man yen desu

4 七百円です。
nana hyaku yen desu

### 1 Warm up

Say "Can you give me the receipt?".
(pp.68–9)

Ask "Do you have any cakes?" (pp.18–19)

# Yakkyoku de
## *At the chemist*

To describe an ailment you can use the phrase **…ga shimasu** *("I have…")*, for example **zutsu ga shimasu** *("I have a headache")*, or you could say **…ga itai desu** *("I have a pain in my…")*. Notice that the ailment or part of the body comes first in the sentence.

## 2 Match and repeat

Match the numbered items to the Japanese words in the panel on the left and test yourself using the cover flap.

1 包帯
hohtai

2 シロップ
shiroppu

3 目薬
megusuri

4 絆創膏
bansohkoh

5 注射器
chu-sha ki

6 錠剤
jyohzai

7 座薬
zayaku

8 軟膏
nankoh

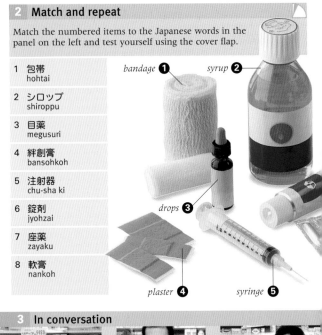

*bandage* ❶  *syrup* ❷

*drops* ❸

*plaster* ❹  *syringe* ❺

## 3 In conversation

こんにちは。
どうしましたか？
konnichiwa.
doh shimashitaka

*Hello. What's the matter?*

腹痛がします。
fukutsu ga shimasu

*I have a stomachache.*

下痢気味ですか？
geri gimi desuka

*Do you also have diarrhoea?*

## 4 Words to remember

Familiarize yourself with these words and test yourself using the flap.

| | | |
|---|---|---|
| *headache* | 頭痛 | zutsu |
| *stomachache* | 腹痛 | fukutsu |
| *diarrhoea* | 下痢 | geri |
| *cold* | 風邪 | kaze |
| *cough* | せき | seki |
| *sunburn* | 日焼け | hiyake |
| *toothache* | 歯痛 | ha-ita |

頭痛がします。
zutsu ga shimasu
*I have a headache.*

## 6 Say it

I have a toothache.

I have a cough.

Do you you have that
as an ointment?

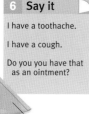

**8** ointment

**7** suppository

**6** tablet

## 5 Useful phrases

Learn these phrases and then test yourself
using the cover flap.

| | |
|---|---|
| *I have a pain in my leg.* | 脚が痛いです。<br>ashi ga itai desu |
| *Do you have that as a syrup?* | それのシロップは<br>ありますか？<br>sore no shiroppu wa<br>arimasuka |
| *I'm allergic to penicillin.* | ペニシリンに対してア<br>レルギー体質です。<br>penishirin ni taishite<br>arerugih taishitsu desu |

いいえ、でも頭痛
がします。
ihe, demo zutsu ga
shimasu

*No, but I have a
headache.*

これをお飲み下さい。
kore o onomi kudasai

*Take this.*

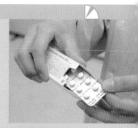

それの錠剤はあり
ますか？
sore no jyohzai wa
arimasuka

*Do you have that as
tablets?*

**1  Warm up**

Say " I have a toothache" and "I have a pain in my leg". (pp.88–9)

Ask politely "What's the matter?" (pp.88–9)

# Karada
## *The body*

Spoken Japanese uses the same pronunciation for leg and foot: **ashi**. However, the written characters are different. There are two separate words describing the back area: *lower back* is **koshi**; *upper back* is **senaka**. Remember there is no plural, so **meh** is *eye* or *eyes*.

## 2  Match and repeat: body

Match the numbered parts of the body with the list on the left. Test yourself by using the cover flap.

1  手
  te

2  頭
  atama

3  肩
  kata

4  肘
  hiji

5  髪
  kami

6  腕
  ude

7  首
  kubi

8  胸
  mune

9  お腹
  onaka

10  脚
  ashi

11  膝
  hiza

12  足
  ashi

*hand* ❶

❹ *elbow*

❺ *hair*

*head* ❷

❻ *arm*

❼ *neck*

❽ *chest*

*shoulder* ❸

❾ *stomach*

❿ *leg*

⓫ *knee*

⓬ *foot*

## 3  Match and repeat: face

Match the numbered facial features with the list on the right.

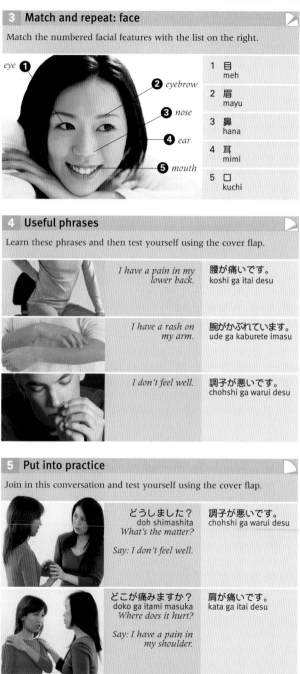

eye ❶

❷ eyebrow

❸ nose

❹ ear

❺ mouth

| | | |
|---|---|---|
| 1 | 目 | meh |
| 2 | 眉 | mayu |
| 3 | 鼻 | hana |
| 4 | 耳 | mimi |
| 5 | 口 | kuchi |

## 4  Useful phrases

Learn these phrases and then test yourself using the cover flap.

| | | |
|---|---|---|
| *I have a pain in my lower back.* | 腰が痛いです。 | koshi ga itai desu |
| *I have a rash on my arm.* | 腕がかぶれています。 | ude ga kaburete imasu |
| *I don't feel well.* | 調子が悪いです。 | chohshi ga warui desu |

## 5  Put into practice

Join in this conversation and test yourself using the cover flap.

どうしました？
doh shimashita
*What's the matter?*

*Say: I don't feel well.*

調子が悪いです。
chohshi ga warui desu

どこが痛みますか？
doko ga itami masuka
*Where does it hurt?*

*Say: I have a pain in my shoulder.*

肩が痛いです。
kata ga itai desu

## Isha to
## *With the doctor*

Say "I have a headache". (pp.88–9)

Now, say "I have a pain in my ear". (pp.90–1)

Ask "What's the matter?" (pp.88–9)

Most Japanese doctors are based in hospitals rather than in separate clinics. You will usually need to go to a hospital for an appointment, even for minor ailments. Many Japanese doctors speak good English, but you could need to give a basic explanation in Japanese, for example, to a receptionist.

**2** Useful phrases you may hear

Learn these phrases and then test yourself using the cover flap to conceal the Japanese on the left.

大したことは
ありません。
taishitakoto wa
arimasen
*It's not serious.*

検査が必要です。
kensa ga hitsuyoh
desu
*Tests are needed.*

骨折です。
kossetsu desu
*You have a fracture.*

入院が必要です。
nyu-in ga hitsuyoh
desu
*You need to stay in hospital. ("Hospital is needed.")*

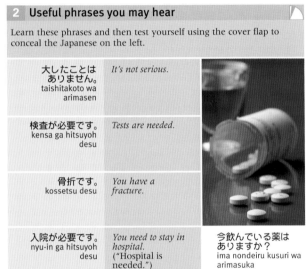

今飲んでいる薬は
ありますか？
ima nondeiru kusuri wa
arimasuka
*Are you taking any medication?*

**3** In conversation

どうしましたか？
doh shimashitaka

*What's the matter?*

胸が痛いです。
mune ga itai desu

*I have a pain in my chest.*

診察しましょう。
shinsatsu shimashoh

*I'll need to examine you.*

> 🔘 **Cultural tip** There are two separate emergency numbers in Japan depending on which service you require. For the police dial 110, for ambulance and fire service dial 119.

## 4 Useful phrases you may need to say

Learn these phrases and then test yourself using the cover flap.

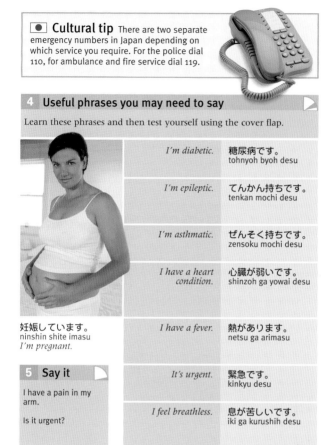

|  |  |
|---|---|
| *I'm diabetic.* | 糖尿病です。<br>tohnyoh byoh desu |
| *I'm epileptic.* | てんかん持ちです。<br>tenkan mochi desu |
| *I'm asthmatic.* | ぜんそく持ちです。<br>zensoku mochi desu |
| *I have a heart condition.* | 心臓が弱いです。<br>shinzoh ga yowai desu |
| *I have a fever.* | 熱があります。<br>netsu ga arimasu |
| *It's urgent.* | 緊急です。<br>kinkyu desu |
| *I feel breathless.* | 息が苦しいです。<br>iki ga kurushih desu |

妊娠しています。
ninshin shite imasu
*I'm pregnant.*

## 5 Say it

I have a pain in my arm.

Is it urgent?

---

重い病気ですか？
omoi byohki desuka

*Is it serious?*

いいえ、ただの消化
不良です。
ihe, tadano shohka
furyoh desu

*No, you only have indigestion.*

よかった！安心し
ました。
yokatta. anshin
shimashita

*Good! What a relief.*

## 1 Warm up

Say "Where's the florist?" (pp.68–9)

Say "Tests are needed". (pp.92–3)

What is the Japanese for "mouth" and "head"? (pp.90–1)

# Byoh-in de
## *In hospital*

It is useful to know a few basic Japanese phrases relating to hospitals for use in an emergency or in case you need to visit a friend or colleague in hospital. Japanese medical care is excellent but very expensive, so make sure you have adequate insurance.

## 2 Useful phrases

Familiarize yourself with these phrases. Conceal the Japanese with the cover flap and test yourself.

| | |
|---|---|
| 待合室はどこですか？<br>machiai shitsu wa doko desuka | *Where's the waiting room?* |
| どのくらいかかりますか？<br>dono kurai kakari masuka | *How long does it take?* |
| 痛いですか？<br>itai desuka | *Will it hurt?* |
| ベッドに横になってください。<br>beddo ni yoko ni natte kudasai | *Please lie down on the bed.* |
| 六時間何も食べないでください。<br>roku jikan nanimo tabenaide kudasai | *Please do not eat anything for six hours.* |
| 頭を動かさないでください。<br>atama o ugokasanai de kudasai | *Don't move your head.* |
| 口を開けてください。<br>kuchi o akete kudasai | *Open your mouth.* |
| 血液検査が必要です。<br>ketsueki kensa ga hitsuyoh desu | *A blood test is needed.* |

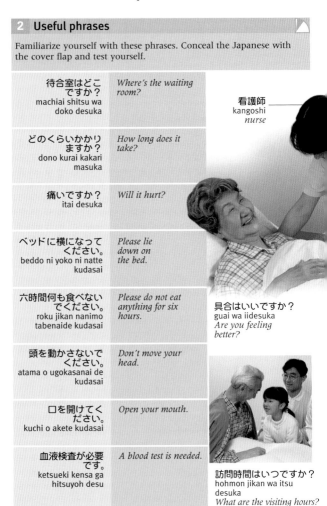

看護師
kangoshi
*nurse*

具合はいいですか？
guai wa iidesuka
*Are you feeling better?*

訪問時間はいつですか？
hohmon jikan wa itsu desuka
*What are the visiting hours?*

## 3 Words to remember

Memorize these words and test yourself using the cover flap.

| | |
|---|---|
| *emergency ward* | 緊急病棟<br>kinkyu byohtoh |
| *children's ward* | 小児病棟<br>shohni byohtoh |
| *operating theatre* | 手術室<br>shujyutsu shitsu |
| *waiting room* | 待合室<br>machiai shitsu |
| *corridor* | 廊下<br>rohka |
| *stairs* | 階段<br>kaidan |
| *lift* | エレベーター<br>erebehtah |

レントゲンは正常
です。
rentogen wa seijyoh desu
*The x-ray is normal.*

## 4 Put into practice

Join in this conversation. Read the Japanese on the left and follow
the instructions to make your reply. Then test yourself by hiding the
answers with the cover flap.

大したことは
ありません。
taishitakoto wa
arimasen
*It's not serious.*

Ask: Are tests needed?

検査が必要ですか？
kensa ga hitsuyoh
desuka

血液検査が必要
です。
ketsueki kensa ga
hitsuyoh desu
*A blood test is needed.*

Ask: Will it hurt?

痛いですか？
itai desuka

## 5 Say it

Is a blood test
needed?

Where's the children's
ward?

An x-ray is needed.

**● Read it** It's useful to be able to
recognize the Japanese for "hospital". This
literally means "sick building". The first
character 病 **byoh** can also be found in other
words such as 病気 **byoh-ki**, "sickness", and
病人 **byoh-nin**, "sick person" or "patient".

病院 *byoh-in* hospital

**Kotae**
*Answers*
Cover with flap

# Fukushu to kurikaesh
## Review and repeat

## 1 The body

1 頭
  atama

2 腕
  ude

3 胸
  mune

4 お腹
  onaka

5 脚
  ashi

6 膝
  hiza

7 足
  ashi

### 1 The body

Name the numbered body parts in Japanese.

- 1 head
- 2 arm
- chest 3
- 4 stomach
- leg 5
- knee 6
- foot 7

## 2 On the phone

1 大和さんお願い
  します。
  Yamato-san
  onegai shimasu

2 ゴープレス・
  プリンターのジ
  ャック・ハント
  と申します。
  Gopress purintah
  no Jack Hunt to
  mohshimasu

3 メッセージを伝
  えていただけま
  すか？
  messehji o
  tsutaete itadake
  masuka

4 ミーティングは
  火曜日ではあり
  ません。
  mihtingu wa kayoh
  bi dewa arimasen

5 ありがとうござ
  います。
  arigatoh gozaimasu

### 2 On the phone

You are arranging an appointment. Follow the conversation, replying in Japanese following the English prompts.

moshi moshi, japanihzu konekushon desu
1 *I'd like to speak to Mr Yamato.*

dochira sama desuka
2 *Jack Hunt of Gopress Printers.*

sumimasenga, ima hanashichu desu
3 *Can I leave a message?*

mochiron desu
4 *The meeting isn't on Tuesday.*

wakarimashita
5 *Thank you very much.*

## 3 Clothing

Say the Japanese words for the numbered items of clothing.

*jacket* ❶

*tie* ❷

❶ (jacket)

*trousers* ❸

❻ *skirt*

*shoes* ❹  *tights* ❺

### 3 Clothing

1 ジャケット
jyaketto

2 ネクタイ
nekutai

3 パンツ
pantsu

4 靴
kutsu

5 ストッキング
sutokkingu

6 スカート
sukahto

## 4 At the doctor's

Say these phrases in Japanese.

1 *I have a pain in my leg.*

2 *Is it serious?*

3 *I have a heart condition.*

4 *Will it hurt?*

5 *I'm pregnant.*

### 4 At the doctor's

1 脚が痛いです。
ashi ga itai desu

2 重い病気ですか？
omoi byohki desuka

3 心臓が弱いです。
shinzoh ga yowai desu

4 痛いですか？
itai desuka

5 妊娠しています。
ninshin shite imasu

## 1 Warm up

Say the months of the year in Japanese. (pp.28–9)

Ask "Is there a museum in town?" (pp.48–9) and "How much is that?" (pp.18–19)

# Ie
## *Home*

In Japan space is limited and most city-dwellers live in apartments (**aparto** or the more luxurious **manshon**). Rooms are often small and a combined kitchen and dining room (**dainingu kitchin**) is common. Earthquakes are frequent and buildings have to comply with strict specifications.

## 2 Match and repeat

Match the numbered items to the list and test yourself using the flap.

1 雨どい
amadoi

2 バルコニー
barukonih

3 窓
mado

4 雨戸
amado

5 屋根
yane

6 壁
kabe

7 ドア
doa

8 階段
kaidan

9 庭
niwa

**1** gutter  **2** balcony  window **3**

garden **9**  steps **8**  door **7**

**Cultural tip** In addition to being built to withstand earthquakes, most Japanese buildings have steel or wooden anti-typhoon shutters. These can be closed quickly to seal off the house or apartment from raging winds and rain. The hurricane and typhoon season lasts from late August to early October, although storms can occur outside these months.

## 3  Words to remember

Familiarize yourself with these words and test yourself using the flap.

家賃は一月いくら
ですか？
yachin wa hitotsuki
ikura desuka
*How much is the rent
per month?*

| | |
|---|---|
| *room* | 部屋<br>heya |
| *floor* | 床<br>yuka |
| *ceiling* | 天井<br>ten-jyoh |
| *bedroom* | 寝室<br>shinshitsu |
| *bathroom* | バスルーム<br>basu ru-mu |
| *kitchen* | 台所<br>daidokoro |
| *dining room* | ダイニングルーム<br>dainingu ru-mu |
| *living room* | 居間<br>ima |
| *attic* | 屋根裏<br>yane ura |
| *parking space* | 車庫<br>shako |

**4** *shutter*  **5** *roof*

**6** *wall*

## 4  Useful phrases

Learn these phrases and test yourself.

*Is there a parking
space?*

車庫はありますか？
shako wa arimasuka

*When can I move in?*

いつ入居できま
すか？
itsu nyu-kyo
dekimasuka

## 5  Say it

Is there a dining
room?

Where's the attic?

It's furnished.

*Is it furnished?*

家具付きですか？
kagu tsuki desuka

## 1 Warm up

What's the Japanese for "table" (pp.20–1), "desk" (pp.80–1), "bed" (pp.60–1), and "curtains"? (pp.60–1)

How do you say "This car is small?" (pp.64–5)

# Ie no naka de
## *Inside the home*

The Japanese often end their sentences with short "markers" that don't change the meaning but carry different nuances. For example, the **yo** marker can imply *"and even"* or *"to be sure"* and **ne** can mean something like *"isn't that so?"*. You'll see examples of these in the conversation below.

## 2 Match and repeat

Match the numbered items to the list in the panel on the left. Then test yourself by concealing the Japanese with the cover flap.

1 流し
nagashi

2 蛇口
jyaguchi

3 炊飯器
sui-hanki

4 調理台
chohridai

5 食器洗い機
shokki araiki

6 椅子
isu

7 戸棚
todana

8 テーブル
tehburu

❶ *sink*  ❷ *tap*

❺ *dishwasher*  *chair* ❻  *cabinet* ❼  *table* ❽

## 3 In conversation

これが冷蔵庫です。
kore ga reizohko desu

*This is the fridge.*

炊飯器はありますか？
sui-hanki wa arimasuka

*Is there a rice cooker?*

はい、そしてこれがレンジです。
hai, soshite kore ga renji desu

*Yes, and here's the stove.*

## 4 Words to remember

Familiarize yourself with these words and test yourself using the flap.

| | | |
|---|---|---|
| *sofa* | ソファ | sofa |
| *carpet* | 絨毯 | jyu-tan |
| *bath* | バス | basu |
| *toilet* | トイレ | to-ee-reh |
| *stove* | レンジ | renji |
| *washing machine* | 洗濯機 | sentaku ki |
| *fridge* | 冷蔵庫 | reizohko |

このソファは新しいです。
kono sofa wa atarashih
desu
*This sofa is new.*

**3** *rice cooker*

**4** *worktop*

## 5 Useful phrases

Learn these phrases and then test yourself using the cover flap to conceal the Japanese.

| | |
|---|---|
| *The fridge is broken.* | 冷蔵庫が壊れています。 reizohko ga kowarete imasu |
| *I'm not fond of the curtains.* | カーテンが気に入りません。 kahten ga kini irimasen |
| *Are heat and electricity included?* | 光熱費込みですか？ kohnetsu hi komi desuka |

## 6 Say it

Is there a washing machine?

The fridge is new.

The tap is broken.

流しが新しいですね。
nagashi ga atarashih
desune

*The sink is new.*

それから食器洗い機もありますよ。
sorekara shokki araiki
mo arimasuyo

*And there's even a dishwasher.*

なんてきれいなタイルなんでしょう！
nante kireh na tairu
nandeshoh

*What pretty tiles!*

## 1 Warm up

What's the Japanese for "day" and "month"? (pp.28–9)

Say "Where's the florist?" (pp.68–9) and "Is there a garden?" (pp.98–9)

# Niwa
## *The garden*

Japanese gardens, often with water features and plants like lilies and cherry trees, can be seen in public places such as parks, temples, and hotels. Space constraints mean that many Japanese homes don't have their own gardens, but house plants and flower arrangements are popular.

## 2 Words to remember

Familiarize yourself with these words and test yourself using the flap.

| | |
|---|---|
| 冬 fuyu | *winter* |
| 春 haru | *spring* |
| 夏 natsu | *summer* |
| 秋 aki | *autumn* |

❷ *tree*

❸ *plants*

*waterfall* ❶

*flowers* ❿

*stones* ❾   *rocks* ❽

## 3 Useful phrases

Learn these phrases and then test yourself using the cover flap.

| | | |
|---|---|---|
| | *What kind of tree is this?* | これは何の木<br>ですか？<br>kore wa nanno ki<br>desuka |
| | *I like the pond.* | 池が好きです。<br>ike ga suki desu |
| | *What beautiful flowers!* | きれいな花ですね！<br>kireh na hana desune |
| | *Can we walk in the garden?* | 庭を歩いてい<br>いですか？<br>niwa o aruite ihdesuka |

## 4 Match and repeat

Match the numbered items to the words in the panel on the right.

**4** *soil*

**5** *path*

**6** *grass*

*pond* **7**

### 5 Say it

What kind of flower is this?

I like the waterfall.

Is there a pond?

| | | |
|---|---|---|
| 1 | 滝 | taki |
| 2 | 木 | ki |
| 3 | 植物 | shokubutsu |
| 4 | 土 | tsuchi |
| 5 | 小道 | komichi |
| 6 | 草 | kusa |
| 7 | 池 | ike |
| 8 | 岩 | iwa |
| 9 | 石 | ishi |
| 10 | 花 | hana |

### 1 Warm up

Say "My name is John". (pp.8–9)

Say "I like the pond". (pp.102–3)

What's "fish" in Japanese? (pp.22–3)

# Dohbutsu
## *Animals*

The Japanese tend to keep small lap dogs and sometimes cats in the house as pets. There is not usually enough space indoors for larger animals. Reptiles and insects, such as snakes and crickets, are also popular, particularly amongst young boys.

### 2 Match and repeat

Match the numbered animals to the Japanese words in the panel on the left. Then test yourself using the cover flap.

1 猫
  neko

2 鳥
  tori

3 魚
  sakana

4 犬
  inu

5 馬
  uma

cat ❶

bird ❷

fish ❸

dog ❹

❺ horse

### 3 Useful phrases

Learn these phrases and then test yourself using the cover flap.

| | |
|---|---|
| この犬はおとなしいですか？<br>kono inu wa otonashih desuka | *Is this dog friendly?* |
| 名前は何ですか？<br>namae wa nandesuka | *What's his name?* |
| 猫は苦手です。<br>neko wa negate desu | *I'm not keen on cats.* |
| この犬は噛みつきませんよ。<br>kono inu wa kamitsuki masenyo | *This dog doesn't bite.* |

あなたの猫ですか？
anata no neko desuka
*Is this your cat?*

**Cultural tip** Some buildings will keep larger dogs outside as guard dogs. Native Japanese dog breeds, such as the Kishuken, Shibaken and Ainuken, are known for their toughness and are employed as "yard" dogs rather than treated as pets.

猛犬に注意
Beware of the Dog

### 4 Words to remember

Familiarize yourself with these words and test yourself using the flap.

| | | |
|---|---|---|
| *monkey* | 猿 | saru |
| *sheep* | 羊 | hitsuji |
| *cow* | 牛 | ushi |
| *pig* | 豚 | buta |
| *rabbit* | 兎 | usagi |
| *mouse* | ネズミ | nezumi |

あれは何という魚
ですか？
a-re wa nanto yu sakana
desuka
*What's that fish
called?*

**Read it** Most basic words referring to natural features or animals, such as "tree", "dog", "flower", "cow", etc., are written in kanji – often with just a single character. Look at the kanji for animals on this page and see if you can spot them in the example phrases.

### 5 Put into practice

Join in this conversation. Read the Japanese on the left and follow the instructions to make your reply. Then test yourself by concealing the answers with the cover flap.

あなたの犬ですか？
anata no inu desuka
*Is this your dog?*

Say: Yes, his name is
Ichiroh.

はい、イチローとい
います。
hai, Ichiroh to ihmasu

犬は苦手です。
inu wa negate desu
*I'm not keen on dogs.*

Say: Don't worry.
He's friendly.

大丈夫です。
おとなしいですよ。
daijyohbu desu.
otonashih desu yo.

# Fukushu to kurikaeshi
*Review and repeat*

## 1 Colours

1 白
  shiro

2 黄色
  ki iro

3 緑
  midori

4 黒
  kuro

5 赤
  aka

6 青
  ao

7 ピンク
  pinku

## 1 Colours

What are these colours in Japanese?

1 *white*      5 *red*

2 *yellow*     6 *blue*

3 *green*      7 *pink*

4 *black*

## 2 Kitchen

1 調理台
  chohridai

2 流し
  nagashi

3 蛇口
  jyaguchi

4 炊飯器
  sui-hanki

5 食器洗い機
  shokki araiki

6 椅子
  isu

7 戸棚
  todana

8 テーブル
  tehburu

## 2 Kitchen

Say the Japanese words for the numbered items.

❶ *worktop*    *sink* ❷    ❸ *tap*

*dishwasher* ❺    *chair* ❻    *cabinet* ❼

## 3 House

You are visiting a house in Japan. Join in the conversation, replying in Japanese where you see the English prompts.

basu ru-mu wa kochira desu
1 *What pretty tiles!*

daidokoro wa ohkih desu
2 *Is there a washing machine?*

hai, sorekara shokki araiki mo arimasuyo
3 *Is there a parking space?*

ihe demo niwa ga arimasu
4 *Is it furnished?*

mochiron desu
5 *How much is the rent per month?*

### 3 House

1 なんてきれいな
タイルなんでし
ょう！
nante kireh na
tairu nandeshoh

2 洗濯機はあり
ますか？
sentaku ki wa
arimasuka

3 車庫はあり
ますか？
shako wa
arimasuka

4 家具付きですか？
kagu tsuki desuka

5 家賃は一月いくら
ですか？
yachin wa hitotsuki
ikura desuka

### 4 At home

Say the Japanese for the following items.

1 *washing machine*

2 *sofa*

3 *attic*

4 *dining room*

5 *tree*

6 *garden*

### 4 At home

1 洗濯機
sentaku ki

2 ソファ
sofa

3 屋根裏
yane ura

4 ダイニング
ルーム
dainingu ru-mu

5 木
ki

6 庭
niwa

④ rice cooker

⑧ table

## 1 Warm up

Ask "How do I get to the station?", and "Where's the post office?" (pp.50–1 and pp.68–9)

What's the Japanese for passport? (pp.54–5)

Ask "What time is it?" (pp.30–1)

# Yu-bin kyoku to ginkoh
## *Post office and bank*

Postcards are a popular form of letter in Japan, especially when sending a New Year greeting. Some postcards are prepaid (the bird and flower pictures work as stamps), so you can post them as soon as you write them.

## 2 Words to remember: post

Familiarize yourself with these words and test yourself using the cover flap to conceal the Japanese on the left.

| 手紙<br>tegami | *letter* |
| 封筒<br>fu-toh | *envelope* |
| 小包<br>kozutsumi | *parcel* |
| エアメール<br>ea mehru | *air mail* |
| 書留郵便<br>kakidome yu-bin | *registered post* |
| 切手<br>kitte | *stamps* |
| 郵便配達人<br>yu-bin haitatsu nin | *postman* |
| ポスト<br>posuto | *post box* |

はがき
hagaki
*postcard*

## 3 In conversation

トラベラーズチェックを両替したいです。
toraberahzu chekku o ryohgae shitai desu

*I'd like to change some traveller's cheques.*

身分証明書をお持ちですか？
mibun shohmehsho o omochi desuka

*Do you have any identification?*

はい、これがパスポートです。
hai, kore ga pasupohto desu

*Yes, here's my passport.*

## 4 Words to remember: bank

Familiarize yourself with these words and test yourself using the cover flap to conceal the Japanese on the right.

クレジットカード
*kurejitto kahdo*
*credit card*

| | | |
|---|---|---|
| | *money* | お金<br>okane |
| | *traveller's cheques* | トラベラーズチェック<br>toraberahzu chekku |
| | *cashier* | 窓口<br>madoguchi |
| | *notes* | 紙幣<br>shiheh |
| | *coins* | 硬貨<br>kohka |
| | *cashpoint* | **ATM**<br>"ATM" |
| | *exchange rate* | レート<br>rehto |

クレジットカードで
払えますか？
*kurejitto kahdo de harae masuka*
*Can I pay with a credit card?*

## 5 Useful phrases

Learn these phrases and then test yourself using the cover flap.

### 6 Say it

I'd like to change some dollars.

Here's my credit card.

Where's the post box?

| | |
|---|---|
| *I'd like to change some money.* | お金を両替したいです。<br>okane o ryohgae shitai desu |
| *What is the exchange rate?* | レートはいくらですか？<br>rehto wa ikura desuka |
| *Where's the cashpoint?* | ATMはどこですか？<br>"ATM" wa doko desuka |

ここにご署名をお願いします。
koko ni goshomeh o onegai shimasu

*Please sign here.*

どんな紙幣をご希望ですか？
donna shihei o gokiboh desuka

*How would you like the notes?*

五千円札をお願いします。
go-sen-yen satsu o onegai shimasu

*5000-yen notes, please.*

### 1 Warm up

What is the Japanese for "The fridge is broken"? (pp.100–1)

What's the Japanese for "today" and "tomorrow"? (pp.28–9)

Say "Thank you very much". (pp. 40–1)

# Shu-ri
*Repairs*

You can combine the Japanese words on these pages with the vocabulary you learned in week 10 to help you explain basic problems and cope with arranging most repairs. Rented accommodation is usually arranged via agents, known as **fudohsanya**. They can also help with problems.

## 2 Words to remember

Familiarize yourself with these words and test yourself using the flap.

| | |
|---|---|
| 配管工<br>haikankoh | *plumber* |
| 電気技師<br>denki gishi | *electrician* |
| 機械技師<br>kikai gishi | *mechanic* |
| 建築家<br>kenchiku ka | *builder* |
| 大工<br>daiku | *carpenter* |
| コンピューター<br>修理店<br>konpyu-tah shu-ri ten | *computer repair shop* |
| 清掃業者<br>seisoh gyohsha | *cleaner* |
| コック<br>kokku | *cook* |

機械技師は必要ない<br>です。<br>kikai gishi wa hitsuyoh<br>nai desu<br>*I need a mechanic.*

## 3 In conversation

おはようございます。<br>山田ですが。<br>ohayoh gozaimasu.<br>Yamada desuga.

*Good morning. This is Mrs Yamada.*

おはようございます。<br>どうかなさいましたか？<br>ohayoh gozaimasu.<br>dohka nasai mashitaka

*Good morning. Is there anything wrong?*

食器洗い機が壊れて<br>います。<br>shokki araiki ga<br>kowarete imasu

*The dishwasher is broken.*

## 4 Useful phrases

Learn these phrases and then test yourself using the cover flap.

| | |
|---|---|
| *Please clean the bathroom.* | バスルームを掃除してください。<br>basu ru-mu o sohji shite kudasai |
| *Can you repair the television?* | テレビを修理してもらえますか？<br>terebi o shu-ri shite mora-e masuka |
| *Can you recommend a good mechanic?* | 良い修理屋を紹介してもらえますか？<br>ih shu-ri ya o shohkai shite mora-e masuka |

これはどこで修理してもらえますか？
kore wa doko de shu-ri shite mora-e masuka
*Where can I get this repaired?*

## 5 Put into practice

Cover up the text on the right and complete the dialogue in Japanese.

CDドライブが壊れています。
CD doraibu ga kowarete imasu
*Your CD drive is broken.*

*Ask: Can you recommend a good computer repair shop?*

良いコンピューター修理店を紹介してもらえますか？
ih konpyu-tah shu-ri ten o shohkai shite mora-e masuka

今日中に修理できるでしょう。
kyohjyu-ni shu-ri dekiru deshoh
*It's possible to repair it today.*

街に一店あります。
machi ni itten arimasu
*There's one in the town.*

*Say: Thank you very much.*

どうもありがとうございます。
dohmo arigatoh gozaimasu

修理担当者を送ります。
shu-ri tantoh sha o okuri masu

*We'll send a repair man.*

今日中に来てくれますか？
kyohjyu ni kite kure masuka

*Can you do it today?*

すみません。明日の朝になります。
sumimasen. ashita no asa ni narimasu

*Sorry. But it will be tomorrow morning.*

Say the days of the week in Japanese. (pp.28–9)

How do you say "cleaner"? (pp.110–11)

Say "It's 9.30", "10.45", and "12.00". (pp.30–1)

# Kuru
## *To come*

Japanese verbs don't generally change with the subject, but do take different endings according to the tense or "mood" (see pp.40–1). Below you will see some of these changes for the verb **kuru** *(to come)* with examples, including the useful **ki-te** form used for invitations.

## **2** **Useful phrases**

Say the different forms of **kuru** *(to come)* aloud. Use the cover flap to test yourself and, when you are confident, practice the sample sentences below.

| | |
|---|---|
| 来る<br>kuru | *to come*<br>*(infinitive)* |
| 来ます<br>kimasu | *come/coming*<br>*(present)* |
| 来ません<br>kimasen | *not come/coming*<br>*(present negative)* |
| 来ました<br>kimashita | *came*<br>*(past)* |
| 来ませんでした<br>kimasen deshita | *didn't come*<br>*(past negative)* |
| 来て<br>ki-te | *come!*<br>*(invitation)* |
| バスが来ません。<br>basu ga kimasen | *The bus isn't coming.* |
| 大工さんは九時に<br>来ました。<br>daikusan wa kuji ni<br>kimashita | *The carpenter came*<br>*at nine o'clock.* |
| 清掃業者は今日は<br>来ませんでした。<br>sehsoh gyohsha wa kyoh<br>wa kimasen deshita | *The cleaner didn't*<br>*come today.* |
| 明日来るつもりです。<br>ashita kuru tsumori desu | *I intend to come*<br>*tomorrow.* |

彼らは電車で来ます。
karera wa densha de kimasu
*They're coming*
*by train.*

**●** **Conversational tip** Beware of English phrases using "come" that translate differently in Japanese. For example, the Japanese equivalent of "I come from Australia" would be "ohsutoraria jin desu", which translates literally as "Australia person I am".

## 3 Invitations

You can use **ki-te** *(come!)* with **kudasai** *(please)* for basic invitations, but there are also different expressions depending on the level of formality.

| | | |
|---|---|---|
| 私の誕生パーティーに来てください。<br>watashi no tanjyoh pahtih ni ki-te kudasai | *Please come to my birthday party.* |
| 月曜日のレセプションにいらしていただけますか？<br>getsuyoh-bi no resepushon ni irashite itadake masuka | *Can you come to our reception on Monday? (formal)* |
| 金曜日のセミナーにお越し願えますでしょうか？<br>kinyoh-bi no seminah ni okoshi negaemasu deshohka | *Would you be able to come to our seminar on Friday? (very formal)* |
| ディナーパーティーに来てね！<br>dinah pahtih ni kitene | *Come to my dinner party! (informal)* |

## 4 Put into practice

Join in this conversation. Read the Japanese on the left and follow the instructions to make your reply. Then test yourself by concealing the answers with the cover flap.

もしもし。<br>moshi moshi<br>*Hello.*

Say: Hello. Please come to my birthday party.

もしもし。私の誕生パーティーに来てください。<br>moshi moshi. watashi no tanjyoh pahtih ni ki-te kudasai

パーティーはいつですか？<br>pahtih wa itsu desuka<br>*When is the party?*

Say: It's tomorrow at eight o'clock.

明日の8時です。<br>ashitano hachi ji desu

はい、ぜひ。<br>hai, zehi<br>*Yes, I'd love to.*

Say: So see you tomorrow.

ではまたあした。<br>dewa mata ashita

## Kehsatsu to hanzai
*Police and crime*

What's the Japanese for "tall" and "short"? (pp.64–5)

Say "The room is big" and "The bed is small". (pp.64–5)

Japanese police cars are black and white with a red strip light on the roof. The uniforms are blue and grey with a peaked cap. Note that the terms **otoko** *(man)* and **onna** *(woman)* in section 4 are not very polite as they refer to criminal suspects. More polite equivalents would be **danseh** and **jyoseh**.

### 2 Words to remember: crime

Familiarize yourself with these words.

| | | |
|---|---|---|
| どろぼう<br>doroboh | *thief/burglar* | |
| 通報<br>tsuh-hoh | *police report* | |
| 報告書<br>hohkoku sho | *statement* | |
| 証人<br>shoh nin | *witness* | |
| 目撃者<br>mokugeki sha | *eye-witness* | |
| 弁護士<br>bengo shi | *lawyer* | |
| 警察官<br>kehsatsu kan | *police officer* | |

弁護士が必要です。
bengo shi ga hitsuyoh desu
*I need a lawyer.*

### 3 Useful phrases

Learn these phrases and then test yourself using the cover flap.

| | | |
|---|---|---|
| すられました。<br>surare mashita | *I've been pick-pocketed.* | カメラ<br>kamera<br>*camera* |
| 何が盗まれました<br>か？<br>nani ga nusumare mashitaka | *What was stolen?* | |
| 犯人を見ましたか？<br>hannin o mimashitaka | *Did you see who did it?* | お金<br>okane<br>*money* |
| いつおこりました<br>か？<br>itsu okori mashitaka | *When did it happen?* | 財布<br>saifu<br>*wallet* |

## 4  Words to remember: appearance

Learn these words and then test yourself using the cover flap.

| | | |
|---|---|---|
| man/men | 男 otoko | |
| woman/women | 女 onna | |
| tall | 背の高い se no takai | |
| short | 背の低い se no hikui | |
| young | 若い wakai | |
| old | 年を取った toshi o totta | |
| fat | 太った futotta | |
| thin | 痩せた yaseta | |
| beard | あごひげ ago hige | |
| moustache | 口ひげ kuchi hige | |
| glasses | 眼鏡 megane | |

男は白髪混じりで眼鏡
をかけていました。
otoko wa shiraga majiri de
megane o kakete imashita
*The man had grey hair
and glasses.*

女は背が高く髪が長か
ったです。
onna wa se ga takaku kami
ga nagakatta desu
*The woman was tall and
had long hair.*

**◉ Read it** The Japanese script for "police" is written with two
kanji characters: 警察 (kehsatsu). Adding the character 官 (kan)
will produce "policeman": 警察官 (kehsatsu kan); and adding
署 (sho) will produce "police station": 警察署 (kehsatsu sho).

## 5  Put into practice

Practice these phrases. Then use the cover flap to hide the text on the
right and follow the instructions to make your reply in Japanese.

男はどんな格好でし
たか？
otoko wa donna
kakkoh deshita ka
*Can you describe him?*
Say: He was short
and fat.

背が低く太っていま
した。
se ga hikuku futotte
imashita

髪は？
kami wa
*And the hair?*

Say: He had grey hair
and a beard.

白髪であごひげを生
やしていました。
shiraga de ago hige o
hayashite imashita

# Fukushu to kurikaeshi
*Review and repeat*

## 1 To come

1 私はバスで来ます。
watashi wa basu de kimasu

2 電気技師は昨日来ました。
denki gishi wa kinoh kimashita

3 私の誕生パーティーに来てください。
watashi no tanjyoh pahtih ni ki-te kudasai

4 清掃業者は木曜日には来ませんでした。
sehsoh gyohsha wa mokuyohbi niwa kimasen deshita

## 1 To come

Put the following sentences into Japanese using the correct form of **kuru** *(to come)*.

1 *I'm coming by bus.*

2 *The electrician came yesterday.*

3 *Please come to my birthday party.*

4 *The cleaner didn't come on Thursday.*

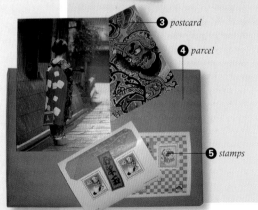

## 2 Bank and post

1 クレジットカード
kurejitto kahdo

2 紙幣
shiheh

3 はがき
hagaki

4 小包
kozutsumi

5 切手
kitte

## 2 Bank and post

Name the numbered items in Japanese.

banknotes **2**

*credit card* **1**

**3** *postcard*

**4** *parcel*

**5** *stamps*

## 3 Appearance

What do these descriptions mean?

1 se ga hikuku yasete imashita

2 otoko wa shohto katto deshita

3 onna wa megane o kakete imashita

4 otoko wa kichi hige o hayashite imashita

5 otoko wa shiraga de ago hige o hayashite imashita

### 3 Appearance

1 He was short and thin.

2 The man had short hair.

3 The woman had glasses.

4 The man had a moustache.

5 He had grey hair and a beard.

## 4 The pharmacy

You are asking a pharmacist for advice. Join in the conversation, replying in Japanese where you see the English prompts.

konnichiwa. doh shimashitaka
1 *I have a stomachache.*

kaze gimi desuka
2 *No, but I have a headache.*

kore o onomi kudasai
3 *Do you have that as a syrup?*

hai, arimasu
4 *How much is that?*

happyaku yen ni narimasu
5 *Thank you.*

### 4 The pharmacy

1 腹痛がします。
fukutsu ga shimasu

2 いいえ、でも
頭痛がします。
ihe, demo zutsu
ga shimasu

3 それのシロップ
はありますか？
sore no shiroppu
wa arimasuka

4 いくらですか？
ikura desuka

5 ありがとう。
arigatoh

## Rejyah
### *Leisure time*

Popular leisure activities outside the house include shopping, playing in the ubiquitous and often very large arcades, or going to karaoke "boxes". New theme parks open regularly and are popular with adults and children alike. Sumo is popular with older people, but theatre and opera are minority pursuits.

<table>
<tr><td>1</td><td>Warm up</td></tr>
</table>

What is the Japanese for "museum" and "cinema"? (pp.48–9)

Say "I like the pond". (pp.103)

Ask "What's your profession?" (p.78–9)

<table>
<tr><td>2</td><td>Words to remember</td></tr>
</table>

Familiarize yourself with these words and test yourself using the cover flap to conceal the Japanese on the left.

| | |
|---|---|
| 劇場 gekijyoh | *theatre* |
| 映画 eiga | *cinema/film* |
| テーマパーク tehma pahku | *theme park* |
| 音楽 ongaku | *music* |
| アート ahto | *art* |
| スポーツ supohtsu | *sport* |
| 旅行 ryokoh | *travelling* |
| 読書 dokusho | *reading* |

歌舞伎が大好きです。
kabuki ga daisuki desu
*I love Kabuki theatre.*

セット
setto
*set*

<table>
<tr><td>3</td><td>In conversation</td></tr>
</table>

カラオケに行きませんか？
karaoke ni ikimasenka

*Do you want to go to a karaoke bar?*

カラオケはきらいです。
karaoke wa kirai desu

*I don't really like karaoke.*

暇なときは何をしていますか？
hima na toki wa nani o shite imasuka

*What do you do in your free time?*

## 4 Useful phrases

Learn these phrases and then test yourself using the cover flap.

ビデオゲームが好き
です。
bideo gehmu ga suki
desu
*I like video games.*

俳優
haiyu
*actor*

| | | |
|---|---|---|
| *What do you do in your free time? (formal)* | 暇なときは何をしていますか？<br>hima na toki wa nani o shite imasuka | |
| *What do you do in your free time? (informal)* | 暇なとき何してる？<br>hima na toki nani shiteru | |
| *My hobby is reading.* | 趣味は読書です。<br>shumi wa dokusho desu | |
| *I prefer the cinema.* | 私は映画の方が好きです。<br>watashi wa eiga no hohga sukidesu | |
| *I hate opera.* | 私はオペラは大嫌いです。<br>watashi wa opera wa daikirai desu | |

舞台
butai
*stage*

## 5 Say it

I like music.

I prefer art.

My hobby is opera.

I hate theme parks.

ショッピングが好き
です。
shoppingu ga suki desu

*I like shopping.*

私はショッピングは
大嫌いです。
watashi wa shoppingu
wa daikirai desu

*I hate shopping.*

良いですよ。一人で
行きます。
ihdesuyo. hitori de
ikimasu

*No problem, I'll go on my own.*

# Supohtsu to shumi
## *Sport and hobbies*

### 1  Warm up

What's the Japanese for "fish"? (pp.104–5)

Say "I like the theatre" and "I prefer travelling". (pp.118–19)

Say "I don't really like...". (pp.118–19)

Traditional Japanese sports include wrestling, martial arts, and fishing. These are still popular, but football, baseball, and golf have also established themselves. Arts and crafts include flower arranging, silk-screen painting, and calligraphy. Participating in tea ceremonies is also a popular hobby.

### 2  Words to remember

Memorize these words and then test yourself.

| | |
|---|---|
| サッカー<br>sakkah | *football* |
| 野球<br>yakyu | *baseball* |
| テニス<br>tenisu | *tennis* |
| 水泳<br>suiei | *swimming* |
| 登山<br>tozan | *mountain climbing* |
| 魚釣り<br>sakana tsuri | *fishing* |
| 絵を描くこと<br>e o kaku koto | *painting* |
| 習字<br>syu-ji | *calligraphy* |

バンカー
bankah
*bunker*

ゴルファー
gorufah
*golfer*

毎日ゴルフを します。
mainichi gorufu o shimasu
*I play golf every day.*

### 3  Useful phrases

Familiarize yourself with these phrases.

| | |
|---|---|
| 野球をします。<br>yakyu o shimasu | *I play baseball.* |
| 彼はテニスをします。<br>kare wa tenisu o shimasu | *He plays tennis.* |
| 彼女は絵を描くこと が好きです。<br>kanojyo wa e o kaku koto ga suki desu | *She likes painting.* |

## 4 Phrases to remember

Learn the phrases below and then test yourself. Notice that "I play" is **shimasu** for sports, but **hikimasu** for musical instruments.

バイオリンを弾きます。
baiorin o hikimasu
*I play the violin.*

フラッグ
furaggu
*flag*

ゴルフコース
gorufu kohsu
*golf course*

| | |
|---|---|
| *What do you like doing? (formal)* | 何をするのがお好きですか？<br>nani o surunoga osuki desuka |
| *What do you like doing? (informal)* | 何をするのが好き？<br>nani o surunoga suki |
| *I like playing golf.* | ゴルフをするのが好きです。<br>gorufu o surunoga suki desu |
| *I like playing baseball.* | 野球をするのが好きです。<br>yakyu o surunoga suki desu |
| *I play tennis.* | テニスをします。<br>tenisu o shimasu |
| *I like going fishing.* | 私は魚釣りが好きです。<br>watashi wa sakana tsuri ga suki desu |
| *I go mountain climbing.* | 登山に行きます。<br>tozan ni ikimasu |

## 5 Put into practice

Learn these phrases. Then cover up the text on the right and complete the dialogue in Japanese. Check your answers.

何をするのがお好きですか？
nani o surunoga osuki desuka
*What do you like doing?*

*Say: Playing football.*

サッカーするのが好きです。
sakkah surunoga suki desu

野球もなさいますか？
yakyu mo nasai masuka
*Do you play baseball as well?*

*Say: No, I play golf.*

いいえ、ゴルフをします。
ihe, gorufu o shimasu

よくプレーなさいますか？
yoku pureh nasai masuka
*Do you play often?*

*Say: Every week.*

毎週です。
maishu desu

## 1 Warm up

Say "(your) husband" and "(your) wife". (pp.12–13)

How do you say "lunch" and "dinner" in Japanese? (pp.20–1)

Say "Sorry, I'm busy that day". (pp.32–3)

# Shakohteki na bamen de
*Socializing*

As a business guest, it's more common to be invited to a restaurant than to someone's home. This is partly practical – people often have long commutes. But if you're staying for longer, you may be invited for a meal or a party.

## 2 Useful phrases

Learn these phrases and then test yourself.

| | |
|---|---|
| ディナーにいらっしゃいませんか？<br>dinah ni irasshai masenka | *Would you like to come for dinner?* |
| 水曜日はいかがですか？<br>suiyoh bi wa ikaga desuka | *What about Wednesday?* |
| また今度誘ってください。<br>mata kondo sasotte kudasai | *Perhaps another time.* |

🔘 **Cultural tip** When visiting a Japanese home, remember that it's usual to remove your outdoor shoes at the door. Take a gift for the host or hostess. Flowers, a bottle of drink or a present from your home country will be very appreciated.

## 3 In conversation

火曜日のディナーにいらっしゃいませんか？
kayoh bi no dinah ni irasshai masenka?

*Would you like to come for dinner on Tuesday?*

すみません。火曜日は忙しいです。
sumimasen. kayoh bi wa isogashih desu

*Sorry. I'm busy on Tuesday.*

木曜日はいかがですか？
mokuyoh bi wa ikaga desuka

*What about Thursday?*

## 4 Words to remember

Familiarize yourself with these words and test yourself using the flap.

招待者
shohtai sha
*hostess*

お客
okyaku
*guest*

| *party* | パーティー<br>pahtih |
| *invitation* | 招待<br>shohtai |
| *gift* | お土産<br>omiyage |

🔲 **Read it** You can now distinguish the three Japanese character sets and recognize some basic recurring words. Use the tables on pp.158–9 to look back over the lessons and see how much more you can read.

## 5 Put into practice

Join in this conversation.

土曜日にパーティーを開くのですが、お暇ですか?
doyoh bi ni pahtih o hiraku no desuga, ohima desuka
*We are having a party on Saturday. Are you free?*

Say: Yes, how nice!

はい、素敵ですね!
hai, suteki desune

ご招待ありがとうございます。
goshohtai arigatoh gozaimasu
*Thank you for inviting us.*

ああよかった!
ah yokatta
*That's great!*

Say: At what time should we arrive?

何時に伺いましょうか?
nanji ni ukagai mashohka

はい、素敵ですね!
hai, suteki desune

*Yes, how nice!*

ご主人もご一緒に。
goshujin mo goissho ni

*Please bring your husband.*

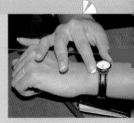

何時に伺いましょうか?
nanji ni ukagai mashohka

*At what time should we arrive?*

# Fukushu to kurikaeshi
*Review and repeat*

**Kotae**
*Answers*
Cover with flap

## 1 Animals

1 猫
neko

2 鳥
tori

3 馬
uma

4 魚
sakana

5 犬
inu

## 1 Animals

Name the numbered
animals in Japanese.

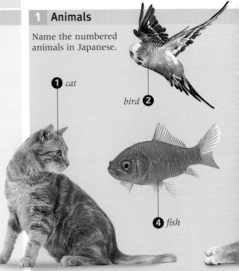

❶ *cat*

*bird* ❷

❹ *fish*

## 2 I like...

1 野球ををするの
が好きです。
yakyu o surunoga
suki desu

2 ゴルフをするの
が好きです。
gorufu o surunoga
suki desu

3 私は絵を描くこ
とが好きです。
watashi wa e o
kaku koto ga suki
desu

## 2 I like...

Say the following in Japanese:

1 *I like playing baseball.*

2 *I like playing golf.*

3 *I like painting.*

**3** horse

**5** dog

### 3 Leisure

What do these Japanese sentences mean?

1 karaoke wa daikirai desu

2 bideo gehmu ga suki desu

3 shumi wa dokusho desu

4 watashi wa gekijyoh no hohga sukidesu

5 baiorin o hikimasu

### 3 Leisure

1 *I hate karaoke.*

2 *I like video games.*

3 *My hobby is reading.*

4 *I prefer the theatre.*

5 *I play the violin.*

### 4 An invitation

You are invited for dinner. Join in the conversation, replying in Japanese following the English prompts.

doyoh bi no dinah ni irasshai masenka
1 *Sorry, I'm busy on Saturday.*

mokuyoh bi wa ikaga desuka
2 *Yes, how nice!*

goshujin mo goissho ni
3 *At what time should we arrive?*

ichi ji han dewa
4 *Thank you very much.*

### 4 An invitation

1 すみません。
土曜日は忙しい
です。
sumimasen.
doyoh bi wa
isogashih desu

2 はい、素敵
ですね！
hai, suteki desune

3 何時に伺いまし
ょうか？
nanji ni ukagai
mashohka

4 ありがとうござ
います。
arigatoh
gozaimasu

# Reinforce and progress

Regular practice is the key to maintaining and advancing your language skills. In this section you will find a variety of suggestions for reinforcing and extending your knowledge of Japanese. Many involve returning to exercises in the book and using the dictionary to extend their scope. Go back through the lessons in a different order, mix and match activities to make up your own 15-minute daily programme, or focus on topics that are of particular relevance to your current needs.

**Keep warmed up**
Re-visit the Warm Up boxes to remind yourself of key words and phrases. Make sure you work your way through all of them on a regular basis.

**1  Warm up**

Ask "How much is that?" (pp.18–19)

What are "breakfast", "lunch", and "dinner"? (pp.20–21)

What are "three", "four", "five", and "six"? (pp.10–11)

**2  I'd like...**

Say you'd like the following:

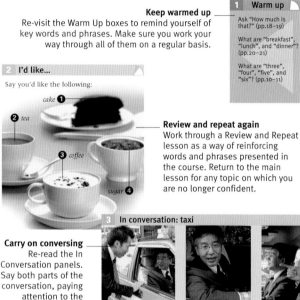

- cake ❶
- ❷ tea
- ❸ coffee
- sugar ❹

**Review and repeat again**
Work through a Review and Repeat lesson as a way of reinforcing words and phrases presented in the course. Return to the main lesson for any topic on which you are no longer confident.

**3  In conversation: taxi**

秋葉原までお願いします。
Akihabara ma-de onegai shimasu

*To Akihabara, please.*

わかりました。
wakarimashita

*Very well.*

ここで降ろしてください。
kokode oroshite ku[

*Can you drop me please?*

**Carry on conversing**
Re-read the In Conversation panels. Say both parts of the conversation, paying attention to the pronunciation. Where possible, try incorporating new words from the dictionary.

**4  Useful phrases**

Learn these phrases and then test yourself using the flap.

| | | |
|---|---|---|
| | What time do you open? | 何時に開きますか？ nanji ni akimasuka |
| | What time does the shop close? | 店は何時に閉まりますか？ mise wa nanji ni shimari masuka |
| | Is wheelchair access possible? | 車いすは使えますか？ kurumaisu wa tsukae masuka |

**Practice phrases**
Return to the Useful Phrases and Put into Practice exercises. Test yourself using the cover flap. When you are confident, devise your own versions of the phrases, using new words from the dictionary.

**Match, repeat, and extend**
Remind yourself of words related to specific topics by returning to the Match and Repeat and Words to Remember exercises. Test yourself using the cover flap. Discover new words in that area by referring to the dictionary and menu guide.

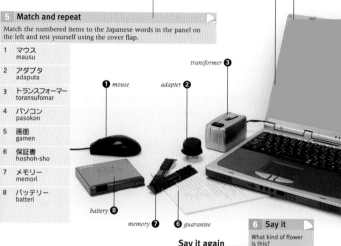

**5  Match and repeat**

Match the numbered items to the Japanese words in the panel on the left and test yourself using the cover flap.

1  マウス
   mausu

2  アダプタ
   adaputa

3  トランスフォーマー
   toransufomar

4  パソコン
   pasokon

5  画面
   gamen

6  保証書
   hoshoh-sho

7  メモリー
   memori

8  バッテリー
   batteri

❹ laptop
❺ screen
transformer ❸
❶ mouse
adapter ❷
battery ❽
memory ❼  ❻ guarantee

**6  Say it**
What kind of flower is this?
I like the waterfall.
Is there a pond?

**Say it again**
The Say It exercises are a useful instant reminder for each lesson. Practise these, using your own vocabulary variations from the dictionary or elsewhere in the lesson.

## Using other resources

In addition to working with this book, try the following language extension ideas:

• Visit Japan if you can and try out your new skills with native speakers. Otherwise, find out if there is a Japanese community near you. There may be shops, cafés, restaurants, and clubs. Try to visit some of these and use your Japanese to order food and drink and strike up conversations. Most native speakers will be happy to speak Japanese to you.

• Join a language class or club. There are usually evening and day classes available at a variety of different levels. Or you could start a club yourself if you have friends who are also interested in keeping up their Japanese.

• Practise your new knowledge of the Japanese scripts and characters (see pp.158–9). Look at the back of food packages and other products. You will often find a Japanese list of ingredients or components. See if you can spot some familiar words in the Japanese list and then compare to the English equivalent.

• Look at the titles and advertisements of Japanese magazines and manga comics. The pictures will help you to decipher the script. Look for familiar words and characters, even if you can't make out the whole text.

• Use the internet to find websites for learning languages, some of which offer free online help.

# Menu guide

This guide lists the most common terms you may encounter on Japanese menus. Dishes are divided into categories and the Japanese script is displayed clearly to help you identify items on a menu.

## Starters and soups

| | | |
|---|---|---|
| hamu | ハム | *ham* |
| ohdoburu | オードブル | *hors d'oeuvres* |
| otsumami | おつまみ | *Japanese appetizer* |
| tsukidashi | つきだし | *Japanese appetizer* |
| ise-ebi | 伊勢えび | *lobster* |
| meron | メロン | *melon* |
| minestorohne | ミネストローネ | *minestrone* |
| kuruma-ebi | 車えび | *prawns* |
| smohku sahmon | スモークサーモン | *smoked salmon* |
| misoshiru | みそ汁 | *soup made with fermented bean paste* |
| tomato supu | トマトスープ | *tomato soup* |

## Egg dishes

| | | |
|---|---|---|
| behkon-eggu | ベーコンエッグ | *bacon and eggs* |
| tamago | 卵 | *egg* |
| medama-yaki | 目玉焼き | *fried eggs* |
| hamu-eggu | ハムエッグ | *ham and eggs* |
| tamago-yaki | 玉子焼き | *Japanese omelette* |
| omuretsu | オムレツ | *omelette* |
| omuraisu | オムライス | *rolled omelette filled with rice* |

| chawan-mushi | 茶碗蒸し | savoury "custard" with egg and fish |
| tamago-dohfu | 卵豆腐 | steamed egg and tofu |

## Fish and sushi

| awabi | あわび | abalone |
| suzuki | すずき／鱸 | sea bass |
| fugu | フグ/河豚 | blowfish |
| katsuo | かつお／鰹 | bonito, tunny |
| unajyu | うな重 | broiled eel on rice |
| koi | コイ／鯉 | carp |
| nami | 並 | cheaper selection of fish |
| hamaguri | はまぐり／蛤 | clam |
| tara | タラ／鱈 | cod |
| tarako | タラコ | cod roe |
| anago | あなご | conger eel |
| kani | かに／蟹 | crab |
| unagi | うなぎ／鰻 | eel |
| joh | 上 | expensive selection |
| unadon | うな丼 | grilled eel on rice |
| nishin | にしん／鰊 | herring |
| kazunoko | かずのこ | herring roe |
| aji | あじ／鯵 | horse mackerel |
| saba | さば／鯖 | mackerel |
| gomoku-zushi | 五目寿司 | mixed "sushi" |
| chirashi-zushi | ちらし寿司 | mixed "sushi" on rice |

| | | |
|---|---|---|
| tako | たこ／蛸 | *octopus* |
| oshi-zushi | 押し寿司 | *Osaka-style "sushi" cut in squares* |
| kaki | カキ牡蠣 | *oyster* |
| sashimi | 刺身 | *raw fish* |
| sushi | 寿司／すし | *raw fish on riceballs* |
| nigiri-zushi | にぎり寿司 | *raw fish on riceballs* |
| sake | さけ／鮭 | *salmon* |
| ikura | イクラ | *salmon roe* |
| iwashi | いわし／鰯 | *sardines* |
| hotategai | ホタテ貝 | *scallop* |
| tai | タイ／鯛 | *sea bream* |
| kappa-maki | カッパ巻き | *seasoned rice and cucumber wrapped in seaweed* |
| inari-zushi | いなり寿司 | *seasoned rice wrapped in fried tofu* |
| uni | うに | *sea urchin* |
| ebi | えび／海老 | *shrimp* |
| nori-maki | のり巻き | *sliced roll of rice, vegetables, and fish powder, wrapped in seaweed* |
| ika | イカ | *squid* |
| ayu | あゆ／鮎 | *sweet smelt* |
| masu | マス／鱒 | *trout* |
| maguro | まぐろ／鮪 | *tuna* |
| kujira | くじら／鯨 | *whale* |
| buri | ブリ／鰤 | *yellowtail* |

## Meat and poultry

| | | |
|---|---|---|
| bahbekyu | バーベキュー | *barbecue* |
| gyu-niku | 牛肉 | *beef* |
| bihfu | ビーフ | *beef* |
| teppan-yaki | 鉄板焼き | *beef and vegetables grilled at the table* |
| gyu-shohgayaki | 牛しょうが焼き | *beef cooked in soy sauce with ginger* |
| bihfu-sutehki | ビーフステーキ | *beef steak* |
| niwatori | 鶏 | *chicken* |
| abaraniku | あばら肉 | *chops/ribs* |
| korokke | コロッケ | *croquettes* |
| tonkatsu | とんかつ | *deep-fried pork cutlets* |
| katsudon | カツ丼 | *deep-fried pork cutlet on rice* |
| kamo | 鴨 | *duck* |
| hireniku | ひれ肉 | *fillet* |
| yakiniku | 焼肉 | *fried pork marinated in soy sauce* |
| kushiyaki | 串焼き | *grilled meat or vegetables on skewers* |
| hanbahgah | ハンバーガー | *hamburger* |
| rebah | レバー | *liver* |
| niku | 肉 | *meat* |
| nikudango | 肉団子 | *meat-filled dumplings* |
| honetsuki | 骨付き | *on the bone* |
| butaniku | 豚肉 | *pork* |

| | | |
|---|---|---|
| buta-shohgayaki | 豚しょうが焼き | *pork cooked in soy sauce with ginger* |
| uzura | うずら | *quail* |
| kareh-raisu | カレーライス | *rice with curry-flavoured stew* |
| rohsuto-bihfu | ローストビーフ | *roast beef* |
| rohsuto-chikin | ローストチキン | *roast chicken* |
| rohsuto-pohku | ローストポーク | *roast pork* |
| sohsehji | ソーセージ | *sausage* |
| sahroin | サーロイン | *sirloin* |
| yakitori | 焼き鳥 | *skewered chicken cooked over a grill* |
| shabu-shabu | しゃぶしゃぶ | *sliced beef with vegetables boiled in a pot at the table* |
| sukiyaki | すき焼き | *sliced beef with vegetables cooked at the table* |
| spearibu | スペアリブ | *spare ribs* |
| suzume | すずめ | *sparrow* |
| stehki | ステーキ | *steak* |

## Rice dishes

| | | |
|---|---|---|
| ...domburi | …丼 | *bowl of rice with something on top* |
| unagidom | うなぎ丼 | *"domburi" with grilled eel* |
| oyakodom | 親子丼 | *"domburi" with chicken and egg* |
| tendon | 天丼 | *"domburi" with deep-fried seafood* |

| tamagodon | 卵丼 | *"domburi" cooked in egg with onions* |
| chyukadom | 中華丼 | *"domburi" with pork and vegetables* |
| nikudon | 肉丼 | *"domburi" with sliced beef* |
| katsudon | カツ丼 | *"domburi" with deep-fried breaded pork cutlet* |
| chah-han | チャーハン | *fried rice* |
| gohan/raisu | ご飯／ライス | *rice* |
| kamameshi | 釜飯 | *rice steamed in fish stock with pieces of meat, fish, and vegetable* |
| chikin raisu | チキンライス | *rice with chicken* |
| onigiri | おにぎり | *rice balls wrapped in seaweed* |

## Noodle dishes

| rahmen | ラーメン | *Chinese noodles* |
| chahshumen | チャーシューメン | *Chinese noodles in pork stock* |
| chanpon | ちゃんぽん | *Chinese noodles in salted stock with meat and vegetables* |
| kanton-men | 広東麺 | *Chinese noodles in salted pork-flavoured soup with vegetables* |
| soba | そば | *long, brownish buck-wheat noodles* |
| udon | うどん | *long, thick, white wheatflour noodles* |

| | | |
|---|---|---|
| sohmen | そうめん | *long, thin, white wheatflour noodles (usually served cold in the summer)* |
| wantan-men | ワンタンメン | *noodle squares (wanton) containing ground pork and leeks, served in soup* |
| tempura soba | 天ぷらそば | *noodles in fish stock with deep-fried shrimps* |
| tsukimi soba | 月見そば | *noodles in fish stock with raw egg on top* |
| niku udon | 肉うどん | *noodles in fish stock with pork or beef* |
| kake soba | かけそば | *simple dish of noodles in fish broth* |
| kitsune udon | きつねうどん | *noodles in fish broth with fried bean curd* |
| chikara udon | 力うどん | *noodles in fish broth with rice cake (mochi)* |
| moyashi soba | もやしそば | *noodles in pork broth with bean sprouts* |
| mori soba | 盛りそば | *noodles served cold, with sweetened soy sauce dip* |
| miso rahmen | 味噌ラーメン | *noodles and pork in bean paste broth* |
| gomoku soba | 五目そば | *soba noodles in broth with pieces of vegetable and meat* |

## Vegetables, seasonings, and salads

| aspara | アスパラ | *asparagus* |
| nasu | なす | *aubergine* |
| takenoko | 竹の子 | *bamboo shoots* |
| tohfu | 豆腐 | *bean curd, tofu* |
| mame | 豆 | *beans* |
| ohitashi | おひたし | *boiled spinach with seasoning* |
| kyabetsu | キャベツ | *cabbage* |
| ninjin | にんじん | *carrot* |
| kyu-ri | キュウリ | *cucumber* |
| miso | 味噌 | *fermented soyabean paste* |
| nattoh | 納豆 | *fermented soyabeans* |
| abura-age | 油揚げ | *fried bean curd* |
| shohga | しょうが | *ginger* |
| pihman | ピーマン | *green pepper* |
| matsutake | 松茸 | *Japanese mushrooms* |
| nori | 海苔 | *dried seaweed* |
| retasu | レタス | *lettuce* |
| mayonehzu | マヨネーズ | *mayonnaise* |
| masshurumu | マッシュルーム | *mushrooms* |
| kinoko | きのこ | *mushrooms (general term)* |
| karashi | からし | *mustard* |
| abura | 油 | *oil* |
| tamanegi | 玉ねぎ | *onion* |
| poteto/ jyagaimo | ポテト／ ジャガイモ | *potatoes* |

| poteto sarada | ポテトサラダ | *potato salad* |
|---|---|---|
| sarada | サラダ | *salad* |
| shio | 塩 | *salt* |
| shiokarai | 塩辛い | *salty* |
| shohyu | 醤油 | *soy sauce* |
| daizu | 大豆 | *soyabeans* |
| hohrensoh | ほうれん草 | *spinach* |
| satoh | 砂糖 | *sugar* |
| amai | 甘い | *sweet* |
| kohn | コーン | *sweetcorn* |
| tomato | トマト | *tomato* |
| yasai | 野菜 | *vegetables* |
| su | 酢 | *vinegar* |
| takuan | タクアン | *yellow radish pickles* |

## *Japanese set meals*

| tehshoku | 定食 | *set meal with rice, soup, pickle, and main dish* |
|---|---|---|
| higawari | 日替わり | *"tehshoku" of the day* |
| tempura | 天ぷら | *"tehshoku" with deep-fried prawns, seafood or vegetables as the main dish* |
| yakiniku | 焼肉 | *"tehshoku" with grilled meat as the main dish* |
| tonkatsu | とんかつ | *"tehshoku" with battered and deep-fried pork cutlet as the main dish* |

| sashimi | 刺身 | *"tehshoku" with raw fish as the main dish* |
| ohiru no | お昼の | *lunchtime "tehshoku"* |
| bentoh | 弁当 | *boxed lunch (sold at railway stations, convenience stores, etc.)* |

## *Fruit and nuts*

| banana | バナナ | *banana* |
| cherih/ sakurambo | チェリー／ さくらんぼ | *cherries* |
| kuri | 栗 | *chestnut* |
| kokonattsu | ココナッツ | *coconut* |
| furu-tsu/ kudamono | フルーツ／ 果物 | *fruit* |
| gurehpu- furu-tsu | グレープフルーツ | *grapefruit* |
| remon | レモン | *lemon* |
| meron | メロン | *melon* |
| orenji | オレンジ | *orange* |
| pihchi/momo | ピーチ／桃 | *peach* |
| kaki | 柿 | *persimmon* |
| painappuru | パイナップル | *pineapple* |
| kiichigo | ラズベリー／木苺 | *raspberry* |
| sutoroberih/ ichigo | ストロベリー／ イチゴ | *strawberries* |
| mikan | みかん | *tangerine* |
| kurumi | クルミ | *walnuts* |
| suika | スイカ | *watermelon* |

## Desserts

| | | |
|---|---|---|
| appuru pai | アップルパイ | *apple pie* |
| kehki | ケーキ | *cake* |
| chihzu-kehki | チーズケーキ | *cheesecake* |
| chokorehto | チョコレート | *chocolate* |
| shu-kurihmu | シュークリーム | *cream puff* |
| kurehpu | クレープ | *crêpe* |
| uji-gohri | 宇治氷 | *crushed ice with green tea syrup* |
| kohri meron | 氷メロン | *crushed ice with melon syrup* |
| dezahto | デザート | *dessert* |
| dohnatsu | ドーナツ | *doughnut* |
| mitsumame | みつ豆 | *gelatine cubes and sweet beans with pieces of fruit* |
| aisukurihmu | アイスクリーム | *ice cream* |
| zerih | ゼリー | *jelly* |
| mochi | もち | *rice cakes (soft and glutinous when ready to eat)* |
| senbeh | せんべい | *rice crackers* |
| manjyu | まんじゅう | *rice-flour buns with bean paste* |
| shahbetto | シャーベット | *sorbet* |
| shohto kehki | ショートケーキ | *"shortcake" (similar to sponge cake)* |
| yohkan | ようかん | *jelly with soft, sweet bean paste filling* |
| sufure | スフレ | *soufflé* |
| kasutera | カステラ | *sponge cake* |

| sutoroberih aisukurihmu | ストロベリー アイスクリーム | *strawberry ice cream* |
|---|---|---|
| oshiruko | おしるこ | *sweet bean soup with rice cake* |
| purin | プリン | *vanilla egg custard with brown sugar* |
| banira aisukurihmu | バニラ アイスクリーム | *vanilla ice cream* |
| kurihmu anmitsu | クリームあんみつ | *vanilla ice cream with seaweed jelly, sweet beans, and fruit* |
| yohguruto | ヨーグルト | *yoghurt* |

## Western snacks

| pan | パン | *bread* |
|---|---|---|
| batah | バター | *butter* |
| chihzu-rohru | チーズロール | *cheese roll* |
| furaido chikin | フライドチキン | *fried chicken* |
| hamusando | ハムサンド | *ham sandwich* |
| jamu | ジャム | *jam* |
| ranchi | ランチ | *lunch* |
| mahmarehdo | マーマレード | *marmalade* |
| piza | ピザ | *pizza* |
| sando icchi | サンドイッチ | *sandwich* |
| spagetti | スパゲッティ | *spaghetti* |
| tohsto | トースト | *toast* |

## Drinks

| nomimono | 飲み物 | *beverages* |
|---|---|---|
| bihru | ビール | *beer* |

| kohcha | 紅茶 | *black tea ("red tea")* |
| kokoah | ココア | *cocoa, hot chocolate* |
| koh-hi | コーヒー | *coffee* |
| kohra | コーラ | *cola* |
| shohchyu | 焼酎 | *Japanese vodka* |
| nama bihru | 生ビール | *draught beer* |
| sohda sui | ソーダ水 | *green, sweet, fizzy drink* |
| ocha/ryokucha | お茶／緑茶 | *Japanese tea* |
| remon tih | レモンティー | *lemon tea* |
| miruk / gyunyu | ミルク／牛乳 | *milk* |
| miruku shehku | ミルクシェイク | *milkshake* |
| mineraru wohtah | ミネラルウォーター | *mineral water* |
| orenji jyu-su | オレンジジュース | *orange juice* |
| orenji sukasshu | オレンジスカッシュ | *orange squash* |
| pain jyu-su | パインジュース | *pineapple juice* |
| sake/nihon-shu | 酒／日本酒 | *rice wine* |
| saidah | サイダー | *fizzy drink* |
| miruku tih | ミルクティー | *tea with milk* |
| tomato jyu-su | トマトジュース | *tomato juice* |
| tonikku wohtah | トニックウォーター | *tonic water* |
| uisukih | ウイスキー | *whisky* |
| onzarokku | オンザロック | *(whisky) on the rocks* |
| mizuwari | 水割り | *(whisky) with water* |

| wain/ budohshu | ワイン／ぶどう酒 | *wine* |
|---|---|---|
| edamame | 枝豆 | *green beans in the pod served as snacks with drinks* |

## Chinese meals

| subuta | 酢豚 | *a kind of sweet-and-sour pork* |
|---|---|---|
| mahboh-dohfu | マーボー豆腐 | *bean curd in spicy meat sauce mixture* |
| chu-ka ryohri | 中華料理 | *Chinese food* |
| harumaki | 春巻き | *deep-fried spring roll* |
| gyohza | 餃子 | *fried dumplings stuffed with minced pork* |
| kurage no | くらげの | *sliced parboiled jellyfish* |
| shu-mai | シュウマイ | *small steamed pork dumplings in thin Chinese filo pastry* |
| niku-man | 肉まん | *steamed dumplings filled with seasoned minced pork* |

## Festival food

| yaki-imo | 焼き芋 | *baked sweet potato* |
|---|---|---|
| watagashi | 綿菓子 | *candy floss* |
| ikayaki | イカ焼き | *charcoal-grilled squid* |
| takoyaki | たこ焼き | *griddle-fried octopus (in batter)* |

| oden | おでん | *hotchpotch of fish and vegetable boiled in fish broth* |
| amaguri | 甘栗 | *roasted chestnuts* |
| tohmorokoshi | とうもろこし | *roasted corn on the cob* |
| okonomiyaki | お好み焼き | *Japanese-style savoury pancakes* |
| tako senbeh | たこせんべい | *shrimp-flavoured pink crackers* |

## Cooking methods and styles

| robatayaki | 炉端焼き | *charcoal-grilled fish and vegetables* |
| okashi | お菓子 | *confectionery* |
| kappoh | 割烹 | *special order Japanese-style dishes* |
| agemono | 揚げ物 | *deep-fried foods* |
| tempura | 天ぷら | *deep-fried seafood and vegetables in batter* |
| nabemono | 鍋物 | *food cooked in a pot at the table* |
| yakimono | 焼き物 | *grilled foods* |
| kaiseki ryohri | 懐石料理 | *Japanese haute cuisine* |
| nihon ryohri/ washoku | 日本料理／和食 | *Japanese-style cuisine* |
| men rui | 麺類 | *noodle dishes* |
| tsukemono | 漬物 | *pickled foods* |

| | | |
|---|---|---|
| tori-ryohri | 鳥料理 | *poultry dishes* |
| kyohdo ryohri | 郷土料理 | *regional specialities* |
| gohan-mono | ご飯もの | *rice dishes* |
| nimono | 煮物 | *simmered foods* |
| shirumono | 汁物 | *soups* |
| mushimono | 蒸し物 | *steamed foods* |
| shohjin ryohri | 精進料理 | *ascetic, monastic style of vegetarian cooking* |
| sunomono | 酢の物 | *vinegared foods* |
| sehyoh ryohri | 西洋料理 | *Western-style cuisine* |

# Dictionary
## *English* to Japanese

The plural is normally the same as the singular in Japanese. In general, Japanese descriptive words, or adjectives, may change depending on how they are used. Some of these adjectives are followed by **(no)** or **(na)**. If a noun is used following such a word then the **no** or **na** must be put after the adjective: **kanojo wa kireh desu** *(she is pretty);* **kanojo wa kireh na jyoseh desu** *(she is a pretty girl).*

## A

*about: about 16* jyu-roku kurai
*accelerator* akuseru
*accident* jiko
*accommodation* heya
*accountant* kaikehshi
*ache* itami
*actor* haiyu
*adapter* (electrical) adaputa
*address* jyu-sho
*admission charge* nyujoh ryoh
*aeroplane* hikohki
*after* ato
*afternoon* gogo
*aftershave lotion* afutah-shehbu-rohshon
*again* mata
*against* hantai
*agenda* kaigi jikoh
*air conditioning* eakon
*air freshener* ea-furesshnah
*air hostess* ea-hosutesu
*air mail* ea mehru
*airline* kohku-gaisha
*airport* ku-koh
*alcohol* arukohru
*all* zembu
    *that's all, thanks* arigatoh, sore de zenbu desu
*almost* hotondo
*alone* hitori de
*already* sudeni
*always* itsmo
*am: I am British* watashi wa igirisu jin desu
*ambulance* kyu-kyu-sha
*America* Amerika
*American* (person) amerika jin
    (adj) amerika no
*and* (with nouns) to
    (with verbs) soshite
*ankle* ashikubi
*anniversary* kinenbi
*anorak* anorakku
*another* (different) betsu (no)
    (further) moh hitotsu (no)

*answering machine* rusuban denwa
*antifreeze* futohzai
*antique shop* kottoh hin ten
*antiseptic* bohfuzai/ shohdokuzai
*apartment* apahto
*appetite* shokuyoku
*apple* ringo
*application form* mohshkomisho
*appointment* (go)yoyaku; apo
*apricot* anzu
*April* shi gatsu
*architecture* (field of study) kenchiku gaku
*are: you are very kind* anata wa totemo shinsetsu desu
    *we are English* watashi tachi wa igirisu jin desu
    *they are Japanese* karera wa nihonjin desu
*arm* ude
*arrivals* tohchaku
*art* ahto; bijutsu
*art gallery* bijutsukan
*artist* geijutsuka
*as: as soon as possible* dekiru dake hayaku
*ashtray* haizara
*Asia* Ajia
*asleep: he's asleep* kare wa nemutte imasu
*asthmatic: I'm asthmatic* zensoku mochi desu
*aspirin* aspirin
*at: at the post office* yu-bin kyoku de
    *at night* yoru
    *at 3 o'clock* san ji ni
*attic* yane ura
*attractive* miryokuteki (na)
*August* hachi gatsu
*aunt* oba(san)
*Australia* Ohsutoraria
*Australian* (person) ohsutoraria jin
    (adj) ohsutoraria no

*automatic* jidoh
*autumn* aki
*away: is it far away?* tohi desuka
    *go away!* atchi e itte
*awful* hidoi
*axe* ono
*axle* shajiku

## B

*baby* akachan
*baby wipes* bebih waipu
*back* (not front) ushiro
    (upper back, body) senaka
    (lower back, body) koshi
*bacon* behkon
    *bacon and eggs* behkon-eggu
*bad* warui
*baker* pan ya
*balcony* barukonih
*ball* bohru
    (dance) butohkai
*ball-point pen* bohru-pen
*banana* banana
*band* (musicians) bando
*bandage* hohtai
*bank* ginkoh
*banknotes* shiheh
*bar* bah
    *bar of chocolate* itachoko
*barber* riyoh in
*bargain* bahgen
*baseball* yakyu
*basement* chika
*basin* (sink) sen-mendai
*basket* kago
*bath* ofuro/basu
    *to have a bath* ofuro ni hairu
*bathing hat* sui-ei boh
*bathroom* basu (ru-mu); ofuroba
*battery* batteri; denchi
*beach* hamabe/kaigan
*beans* mame
*beard* hige
*beautiful* utsukushih

*beauty products* keshoh hin
*because* (da)kara
  *because it is too big* ohki-sugiru kara
*bed* beddo
*bed linen* shitsu to makurakabah
*bedroom* shinshitsu/ beddo ru-mu
*bedspread* beddo supureddo
*beef* gyu-niku
*beer* bihru
*before* mae ni
*beginner* shoshinsha
*behind* ushiro
*beige* behju
*bell* beru
*below* shita
*belt* beruto
*beside* soba
*best* ichiban ih
*better* motto ih
*between* aida ni
*bicycle* jitensha
*big* ohkih
*bikini* bikini
*bill* okanjoh
*bird* tori
*birthday* taniyoh bi
  *happy birthday!* otaniyoh bi omedetoh
  *birthday present* taniyoh bi no purezento
*biscuit* bisketto
*bite* (verb) kamu
  (by insect) mushi sasare
*bitter* nigai
*black* kuro
*blanket* mohfu
*blind* (cannot see) mohmoku (no)
  (on window) buraindo
*blister* mizu-bukure
*blood* ketsueki/chi
  *blood test* ketsueki kensa
*blouse* burausu
*blue* ao
*boat* fune
*body* karada
*boil* (verb: water) wakasu
  (noun: on body) hare-mono
*boiled* yudeta
*bolt* (on door) boruto
*bone* hone
*bonnet* (car) bonn-netto
*book* (noun) hon
  (verb) yoyaku suru
  *bookshop* hon ya
*booking office* kippu uriba
*boot* (car) toranku
  (footwear) bu-tsu
*border* kokkyoh

*boring* tsumaranai
*born: I was born in...*
  (place) watashi wa de umare-mashita
  (year) watashi wa nen ni umare-mashita
*both* ryohhoh
  *both of them* futari tomo
  *both of us* watashi tachi futari
  *both...and... ...to...*
*bottle* bin
*bottle opener* sennuki
*bottom* (of box, sea) soko
*bowl* bohru
*box* hako
*boy* otoko no ko
*boyfriend* bohi-furendo
*bra* burajah
*bracelet* udewa/ buresuretto
*braces* (trousers) zubon-tsuri
*brake* (noun) burehki
  (verb) burehki o kakeru
*branch* (office) shiten
*brandy* burandeh
*bread* pan
*breakdown* (car) koshoh
  (nervous) shinkei-suijaku
*breakfast* chohshoku
*breathe* iki o suru
  *I can't breathe* iki ga dekimasen
*bridge* hashi
*briefcase* kaban
*British* (things) igirisu no
  *the British* igirisu jin
*brochure* panfuretto
*broken* kowareta
  *...is broken* ...ga kowarete imasu
  *broken leg* kossetsu shita ashi
*brooch* burohchi
*brother* (older) onihsan
  (younger) otohto
*brown* cha-iro (no)
*bruise* dabokushoh/ uchimi
*brush* (noun) burashi
*bucket* baketsu
*Buddha* Hotoke
*Buddhism* Bukkyoh
*Buddhist* (noun) Bukkyohto
  (adj) Bukkyoh no
*budget* (noun) yosan
*builder* kenchiku ka
*building* tatemono/biru
*bumper* banpah
*burglar* doroboh/yatoh
*burn* (verb) moyasu
  (noun) yakedo

*bus* basu
*business* shigoto; bijinesu
*businessman* kaisha in
*business card* meishi
*bus station* basu teh
*busy* (person) isogashih
  (crowded) konzatsu shita
*but* demo
*butcher* niku ya
*butter* batah
*button* botan
*buy* kau
*by: by the window* mado no soba
  *by Friday* kinyoh bi ma-de ni
  *by myself* jibun de

# C

*cabbage* kyabetsu
*cabinet* (kitchen) todana
*cable car* kehburu kah
*cable TV* kehbru terebi
*café* kafe/kissaten
*cake* kehki
  *cake shop* kehki ya
*calculator* kehsanki
*call: what's it called?* nan to ihmasuka
*calligraphy* shu-ji
*camera* kamera
*can* (tin) kanzume
  *can I have...?* ...o onegai shimasu
*Canada* Kanada
*Canadian* (person) kanada jin
  (adj) kanada no
*cancer* gan
*candle* rohsoku
*cap* (bottle) futa
  (hat) bohshi
*car* kuruma
*car park* chusha jyo
*carburettor* kyaburetah
*card* (business) meishi
*cardigan* kahdigan
*careful* chu-i-bukai
  *be careful!* ki o tsukete
*carpenter* daiku
*carpet* jyu-tan/kahpetto
*carriage* (train) kyakusha
*carrot* ninjin
*carry-cot* akachan yoh kehtai beddo
*car seat* (for a baby) bebih shihto
*case* (suitcase) su-tsu-kehsu
*cash* (money) genkin
  (coins) kohka/koin
  *to pay cash* genkin de harau
*cashier* (bank, etc.) madoguchi

*cashpoint* "ATM"
*cassette* kasetto
*cassette player* kasetto purehyah
*castle* shiro
*cat* neko
*cave* hora-ana/dohkutsu
*CD drive* CD doraibu
*ceiling* ten-jyoh
*cemetery* bochi
*centre* sentah
*certificate* shohmeisho
*chair* isu
  *swivel chair* kaiten isu
*chambermaid* meido
*change* (noun: money) otsuri
  (verb, general) kaeru
  (verb, transport) norikaeru
*character* (written) ji
*charger* (electrical) chahjyah
*cheap* yasui
*check-in* chekku in
*check-out* (hotel) chekkuauto
  (supermarket) reji
*cheers!* kanpai
*cheese* chihzu
*chemist* (shop) yakkyoku
*cheque* kogitte
*cheque book* kogitte choh
*cherry* sakurambo/cherih
*chess* chesu
*chest* mune
*chewing gum* chu-in-gamu
*chicken* niwatori
*child* kodomo
*children* kodomotachi
  *children's ward* shohni byohtoh
*china* tohki
*China* Chyugoku
*Chinese* (person) chyugoku jin
  (adj) chyugoku no
*chips* poteto-furai
*chocolate* chokorehto
  *box of chocolates* hakozume no chokorehto
*chop* (noun: food) choppu
  (to cut) kizamu
*chopstick rest* ohashi-oki
*chopsticks* ohashi
*Christian name* namae
*church* kyohkai
*cigar* hamaki
*cigarette* tabako
*cinema* eiga kan
*city* toshi/machi
*city centre* chu shingai
*class:* (train)
  *first class* ittoh sha
  *second class* nitoh sha

*classical music* kurasshikku ongaku
*clean* (adj.) kireh (na)
*cleaner* seisoh gyohsha
*clear* (obvious) meihaku (na)
  (water) sumikitta
  *is that clear?* wakari-masuka
*clever* kashikoi
*client* kokyaku
*clock* tokei
  (alarm) mezamashi-dokei
*close* (near) chikai
  (stuffy) iki-gurushih
  (verb) shimeru
  *we close at six o'clock* roku ji ni
*clothes* fuku
*club* kurabu
  (cards) kurabu
*coach* choh-kyori basu
  (of train) kyakusha
*coach station* basu hacchaku jyo
*coat* kohto
*coathanger* hangah
*cockroach* gokiburi
*coffee* koh-hih
*coins* kohka/koin
*cold* (illness) kaze
  (weather) samui
  (food, etc.) tsumetai
*collar* eri
*collection* (stamps, etc.) shu-shu
*colour* iro
*colour film* karah firumu
*comb* (noun) kushi
  (verb) toku
*come* kuru
  *come to my party* pahtih ni kitene
  *come here!* koko ni kinasai
  *I come from…* …jin desu
*compartment* shikiri kyakushitsu
*complicated* fukuzatsu (na)
*computer* konpyu-tah
  *computer repair shop* konpyu-tah shu-ri ten
*concert* ongakukai/konsahto
*conditioner* (hair) rinsu/kondishonah
*conductor* (orchestra) shikisha
*conference* (meeting) konferensu
  (academic) gakkai
*congratulations!* omedetoh
*constipation* bempi
*consul* ryohji
*consulate* ryohjikan
*contact lenses* kontakuto renzu

*contraceptive* hinin-yaku
  (pills) hiningu/kondohmu
*contract* (noun) kehyaku sho
*cook* (person) kokku
  (verb) ryohri suru
*cooking utensils* ryohri-dohgu
*cool* suzushih
*cork* koruku
*corkscrew* sen-nuki
*corner* kado
*corridor* rohka
*cosmetics* keshohhin
*cost* (verb) kakaru
  *what does it cost?* ikura kakari-masuka
*cotton* kotton
*cotton wool* dasshimen
*cough* (noun) seki
*country* (state) kuni
  (not town) inaka
*cousin* itoko
*cow* ushi
*crab* kani
*cramp* keiren
*crayfish* zarigani
*cream* (for face, food) kurihmu
*credit card* kurejitto kahdo
*crime* hanzai
*crisps* chippu
*crossing* (pedestrian) ohdan hodoh
*crowded* konzatsu shita
*cruise* kohkai/kuru-zu
*crutches* matsubazue
*cry* (weep) naku
  (shout) sakebu
*cucumber* kyuri
*cuff links* kafusu botan
*cup* kappu
*cupboard* todana
*curlers* kahrah
*curry* kareh
*curtains* kahten
*customs* zeikan
*cut* (noun) kirikizu
  (verb) kiru

# D

*dad* otohsan
*dairy (products)* nyu seihin
*damp* shimetta
*dance* dansu
*dangerous* abunai
*dark* kurai
*daughter* musume san
  *my daughter* musume
*day* hizuke/hi/nichi
*dead* shinda
*deaf* mimi ga tohi
*dear* (person) shitashih
  (expensive) takai
*December* jyu-ni gatsu
*deck chair* dekki che-ah
*deep* fukai

*deliberately* wazato
*delivery* haitatsu
*dentist* ha-isha
*dentures* ireba
*deodorant* deodoranto
*department* (of company, etc.) bu
*department store* depahto
*departures* shuppatsu
*designer* dezainah
*desk* tsukue/desuku
*develop* (a film) genzoh suru
*diabetic: I'm diabetic* tohnyoh byoh desu
*diamond* (jewel) daiyamondo
(cards) daiya
*diarrhoea* geri
*diary* (record of past events) nikki
(schedule) techoh
*dictionary* jisho
*die* shinu
*diesel* dihzeru
*different* chigau/ betsu (no)
*I'd like a different one* betsu no ga hoshih desu
*difficult* muzukashih
*dining car* shokudohsha
*dining room* dainingu ru-mu; shokudoh
*dinner* yu-shoku/dinah
*directory* (telephone) denwachoh
*dirty* kitanai
*disabled* karada no fujiyu (na)
*dishwasher* shokki araiki
*distributor* (in car) haidenki
*dive* tobikomu
*diving board* tobikomi-dai
*divorced* rikonshita
*do* suru
*doctor* isha
*document* shohsho; dokyumento
*dog* inu
*doll* nin-gyoh
*dollar* doru
*door* doa
*double room* (hotel) daburu ru-mu
(ryokan) hutari-beya
*doughnut* dohnatsu
*down* shita
*drawer* hikidashi
*drawing pin* oshi pin
*dress* (noun) doresu
*drink* (verb) nomu
(noun) nomimono
*drinking water* nomimizu
*drive* (verb) untensuru
*driver* untenshu

*driving licence* unten menkyosho
*drops* (for eyes) megusuri
*dry* kawaita
*dry cleaner* dorai kurihningu ya
*dummy* (for baby) oshaburi
*during: during…* …no aida ni
*dustbin* gomibako
*duster* dasutah
*duty-free* menzei

# E

*each* (every) sorezore
*200 yen each* sorezore ni-hyaku yen desu
*ear* mimi
*early* hayai
*earphones* iyafon
*earrings* iyaringu
*east* higashi
*easy* yasashih/ kantan (na)
*egg* tamago
*eight* hachi
*eighteen* jyu-hachi
*eighty* hachi-jyu
*either: either of them* dochira demo
*either…or…* …ka…
*elastic* (noun) gomuhimo
*elastic band* wagomu
*elbow* hiji
*electric* denki no
*electrician* denki gishi
*electricity* denki
*electronics* denshi-kohgaku
*electronics store* denkiya
*eleven* jyu-ichi
*else: something else* nanika hokano mono
*someone else* dareka hokano hito
*anything else?* nanika hoka ni
*e-mail* (ih)mehru
*e-mail address* (ih) mehru adoresu
*embarrassing* hazukashih
*embassy* taishikan
*embroidery* shishyu
*emerald* emerarudo
*emergency* hijoh
*emergency ward* kyu-kyu byohtoh
*emperor* tennoh
*empty* kara (no)
*end* owari
*engaged* (couple) konyaku shita
(telephone) hanashichu
*engine* (motor) enjin

*engineering* (field of study) kohgaku
*England* Igirisu
*English* igirisu no
(language) eigo
*Englishman* igirisu jin
*Englishwoman* igirisu jin
*enlargement* (of photography) hikinobashi
*enough* jyu-bun
*entertainment* goraku
*entrance* nyu-jyoh guchi/ iriguchi
*envelope* fu-toh
*epileptic: I'm epileptic* tenkan mochi desu
*escalator* esukarehtah
*especially* tokuni
*estimate* (noun) mitsumori
*Europe* Yohroppa
*evening* yu-gata/yoru
*good evening* konbanwa
*every* (morning, day etc) mai-
(all) subete no
*everyone* minna
*everything* minna/ zenbu
*everywhere* doko demo
*executive* (person) jyu-yaku
*exhibition* tenji kai
*example* rei
*for example* tatoeba
*excellent* saikoh/ subarashih
*excess baggage* chohka-nimotsu
*exchange* (verb) kohkan suru
*can I exchange this?* kohkan dekimasuka
*exchange rate* rehto
*excursion* ensoku/ kankoh ryokoh
*excuse me!* shitsurei shimasu/sumimasen
*exit* deguchi
*expensive* takai
*explain* setsumei suru
*extension* (telephone) naisen
(lengthening) kakuchoh
*eye* meh
*eyebrow* mayu

# F

*face* kao
*faint* (unclear) usui/ bonyari shita
(verb) kizetsu suru
*to feel faint* memai ga suru

*fair* (funfair) yu-enchi
  *it's not fair* fukohhei desu
*false teeth* ireba/gishi
*family* kazoku
*fan* (folding fan) sensu
  (electric) senpu-ki
  (enthusiast) fan
*fan belt* fan beruto
*far* toh-i
  *is it far from here?* koko kara toh-i desuka
*Far East* Kyokutoh
*fare* unchin; ryohkin
*farm* nohjoh
*farmer* nohfu
*fashion* fasshon
*fast* hayai
*fat* (of person) futotta
  (on meat, etc.) abura/shiboh
*father* otohsan
  *my father* chichi
*fax machine* fakkusu
*February* ni gatsu
*feel* (touch) sawaru
  *I feel hot* atsui desu
  *I feel like…* …no yoh na ki ga shimasu
*felt-tip pen* feruto pen
*ferry* ferih
*fever* netsu
*fiancé(e)* konyakusha/ fianse
*field* (agricultural) nohara
  *what's your field?* gosenmon wa
*fifteen* jyu-go
*fifty* go-jyu
*fig* ichijiku
*figures* (sales, etc.) gohkeh gaku
*filling* (tooth) ha no jyu-ten
  (sandwich) nakami
*film* (cinema) eiga
  (camera) firumu
*filter* firutah
*finger* yubi
*fire* hi
  (blaze) honoh
*fire extinguisher* shohkaki
*firework* hanabi
*first* saisho (no)
*first aid* ohkyu teate
*first floor* nikai
*fish* sakana
*fishing* sakana tsuri
  *to go fishing* tsuri ni iku
*fishing rod* tsuri zao
*fishmonger* sakana ya
*five* go
*fizzy* tansan no
*flag* hata; furaggu
*flash* (camera) furasshu

*flat* (level) taira (na)
  (apartment) apahto
*flat tyre* panku
*flavour* aji
*flea* nomi
*flight* hikoh(ki)
  *flight number…* …bin
  *flight attendant* kyakushitsu jyohmu in
*flip-flops* zohri
*flippers* hire-ashi
*floor* (of room) yuka
*florist* hana ya
*flour* komugiko
*flower* hana
*flute* furu-to
*fly* (verb) tobu
  (insect) hae
*flyover* rittai kohsa
*fog* kiri
*folk music* minzoku ongaku/fohku myu-jikku
*food* tabemono
*food poisoning* shoku chyudoku
*foot* (on body) ashi
*football* sakkah
  (ball) bohru
*for: for…* …no tame ni
  *for me* watashi no tame ni
  *what for?* nan no tame ni
  *for a week* isshu-kan
*foreigner* gaikoku jin
*forest* mori
*fork* fohku
*fortnight* ni-shu-kan
*forty* yon-jyu
*fountain* funsui
*fountain pen* mannen-hitsu
*four* shi/yon
*fourteen* jyu-yon/jyu-shi
*fourth* yombamme
*fracture* kossetsu
*free* jiyu (na)
  (no cost) muryoh
*freezer* reitohko
*Friday* kin-yoh bi
*fridge* reizohko
*fried* ageta
*friend* tomodachi
*friendly* shitashimi no aru/furendorih na
*front: in front of…* …no mae ni
*frost* shimo
*frozen foods* reitoh shokuhin
*fruit* kudamono/furu-tsu
*fruit juice* furu-tsu jyu-su
*fry* ageru
*frying pan* furai pan
*full* ippai
  *I'm full* onaka ga ippai desu
*full board* shokuji tsuki

*funny* omoshiroi
  (odd) okashih
*furnished: is it furnished?* kagu tsuki desuka
*furniture* kagu

# G

*garage* (parking) shako
  (petrol) gassorin sutando
  (repairs) shu-ri ya
*garden* niwa
*garlic* ninniku
*gate* (airport) tohjyoh guchi/gehto
*gay* (happy) yohki (na)
  (homosexual) homosekusharu
*gear* giya
*gear lever* giya rebah
*geisha* (girl) geisha
*get* (fetch) motte kuru
  *have you got…?* …o omochi desuka
  *to get the train* densha ni noru
*get back: we get back tomorrow* ashita kaerimasu
  *to get something back* kaeshite morau
*get in* (to car etc) noru
  (arrive) tsuku
*get out* (of bus etc) oriru
*get up* (rise) okiru
*gift* omiyage; okurimono
*gin* jin
*girl* onna no ko
*girlfriend* gahrufurendo
*give* ageru
*glad* ureshih
  *I'm glad* ureshih desu
*glass* gurasu
  (for drinking) gurasu
*glasses* megane
*gloss prints* kohtaku no aru purinto
*gloves* tebukuro
*glue* nori
*go* iku
  *where are you going?* doko iku no
  *I'm going to…* …ni ikimasu
*golf* gorufu
*golfer* gorufah
*goggles* suichu megane
*gold* kin
*good* ih
  *good!* yokatta
  *good morning* ohayo gozaimasu
  *good evening* konbanwa
*goodbye* (informal) sayonara; (formal) sayohnara

*government* seifu
*granddaughter* mago-musume
*grandfather* ojihsan
  *my grandfather* sofu
*grandmother* obahsan
  *my grandmother* sobo
*grandson* mago-musko
*grapes* budoh
*grass* kusa
*Great Britain* Igirisu
*green* midori/gurihn
*greengrocer* yao ya
*grey* hai-iro (no)
*grill* guriru
*grilled* yaita
*grocer* (shop)
  shokuryoh hinten
*ground floor* ikkai
*guarantee* (noun)
  hoshoh-sho
  (verb) hoshoh suru
*guide book* gaido bukku
*guided tour* gaido tsuki tsuah
*guitar* gitah
*gun* (rifle) jyu/raifuru
  (pistol) pisutoru
*gutter* amadoi

# H

*hair* kami
*haircut* (for man)
  sanpatsu
  (for woman) katto
*hairdresser* biyoh in
*hair dryer* doraiyah
*hair spray* heya supureh
*half* hanbun
  *half an hour*
  sanjippun
*half board* chohshoku
  to yu-shoku tsuki
*ham* hamu
*hamburger* hanbahgah
*hammer* kanazuchi
*hand* te
*handbag* handobaggu
*hand brake* hando
  burehki
*handkerchief* hankachi
*hand towel* oshibori
*handle* (door) handoru
*handsome* hansamu (na)
*hangover* futsuka-yoi
*happen: when did it
  happen?* itsu okori
  mashitaka
*happy* shiawase (na)
*harbour* minato
*hard* katai
  (difficult)
  muzukashih
*hard lenses* (contact)
  hahdo renzu
*harmony* chohwa/
  hahmonih
*hat* bohshi
*hate: I hate…* watashi
  wa…ga daikirai desu

*have* motsu
  *I have… …wa/ga
  arimasu/imasu;
  …o motte imasu
  I don't have… …wa/ga
  arimasen/imasen;
  …o motte imasen
  can I have…?
  …o kudasai
  have you got…?
  …o omochi desuka
  I have a headache
  zutsu ga shimasu
*hay fever* kafunshoh
*he* kare
*head* atama
*headache* zutsu
*headlights* heddo raito
*head office* honsha
*hear* kiku
*hearing aid* hochohki
*heart* shinzoh
*heart attack* shinzoh
  mahi
*heating* danboh
*heavy* omoi
*heel* kakato
*hello!* konnichiwa
  (on the telephone)
  moshi moshi
*help* (noun) enjo/
  tasuke
  (verb) taskeru
  *help!* taskete
*hepatitis* kan-en
*her: it's her* kanojo
  desu
  *it's for her* kanojo no
  desu
  *give it to her*
  kanojo ni agete
  kudasai
  *her book(s)* kanojo no
  hon
  *it's hers* kanojo no
  (mono) desu
*high* takai
*hill* oka
*him: it's him* kare desu
  *it's for him* kare no
  desu
  *give it to him* kare ni
  agete kudasai
*hire* kariru
*his: his shoe(s)* kare no
  kutsu
  *it's his* kare no (mono)
  desu
*history* rekishi
*hitchhike* hicchi-haiku
*HIV positive* eichi ai bui
  kansensya
*hobby* shumi
*holiday* yasumi
  *public holiday* kyu
  jitsu
*home* ie
*homeopathy* dohshu
  ryoh hoh
*honest* shohjiki (na)
*honey* hachimitsu

*honeymoon* shinkon-ryokoh
*horn* (car) kurakushon
*horrible* osoroshih
*horse* uma
*hospital* byoh-in
*hot* atsui
*hot chocolate* kokoah
*hot water bottle*
  yutampo
*hotel* hoteru
*hour* jikan
*house* ie
*household products*
  katei yo-hin
*housewife* sengyo-shufu
*how?* doh
*how much?* ikura
  desuka
*hundred* hyaku
*hungry: I'm hungry*
  onaka ga suite imasu
*hurry: I'm in a hurry*
  isoide imasu
*hurt: will it hurt?*
  itai desuka
*husband* goshujin
  *my husband* otto

# I

*I* watashi
*ice* kohri
*ice cream* aisukurihmu
*ice lolly* aiskyandeh
*if* moshi
*ignition* tenka sohchi
*ill* byohki
*immediately* suguni
*impossible* fukanoh
*in: in Japan* Nihon ni
  *in Japanese* Nihongo
  de
  *in my room* watashi
  no heya ni
*India* Indo
*Indian* (person) indo
  jin
  (adj) indo no
*indicator* winkah
*indigestion* shohka-furyoh
*infection* kansen
*information* johhoh
*information desk*
  madoguchi
*inhaler* (for asthma,
  etc.) kyu-nyu-ki
*injection* chu-sha
*injury* kega
*ink* inku
*inn* (traditional
  Japanese) ryokan
*insect* mushi
*insect repellent*
  mush-sasare
  yobohyaku
*insomnia* fuminshoh
*insurance* hoken
*interesting* omoshiroi
*internet* intahnetto

*internet café* netto kafeh
*interpret* tsu-yaku suru
*invitation* shohtai
*invoice* (noun) sehkyu-sho
*Ireland* Airurando
*Irish* Airurando no
*Irishman* airurando jin
*Irishwoman* airurando jin
*iron* (metal) tetsu
(for clothes) airon
*ironmonger* kanamono ya
*is: he/she/it is...* kare wa/kanojo wa/sore wa...desu
*island* shima
*it* sore
*itch* (noun) kayumi
*it itches* kayui desu

## J

*jacket* jyaketto
*jacuzzi* jagujih
*jam* jamu
*January* ichi gatsu
*Japan* Nihon
*Japanese* (person) nihonjin
(adj) nihon no
(language) nihongo
*Japanese-style* wafu
*jazz* jazu
*jealous* shitto-bukai
*jeans* jihnzu
*jellyfish* kurage
*jeweller* hohseki shoh
*job* shigoto
*jog* (verb) jogingu suru
*to go for a jog* jogingu ni iku
*joke* johdan
*journey* ryokoh/tabi
*July* shichi gatsu
*jumper* jampah/sehtah
*June* roku gatsu
*just: it's just arrived* chohdo tsuki-mashta
*I've just got one left* hitotsu dake nokotte imasu

## K

*key* kih; kagi
*keyboard* kihbohdo
*kidney* jinzoh
*kilo* kiro
*kilometre* kiromehtoru
*kimono* kimono
*kiss* (noun) kisu
*kitchen* daidokoro
*knee* hiza
*knife* naifu
*knit* amu
*know: I don't know* shirimasen

*Korea* Kankoku
*North Korea* Kita Chohsen
*South Korea* Daikanminkoku
*Korean* (person) kankoku jin
(adj) kankoku no

## L

*label* raberu
*lace* rehsu
*lady* fujin/jyoseh
*lake* mizu-umi
*lamb* kohitsuji
*lamp* ranpu; denki stando
*lampshade* denki stando no kasa
*land* (noun) tochi
(verb) chakuriku suru
*language* gengo
*laptop (computer)* (nohto) pasokon
*large* ohkih
*last* (final) saigo (no)
*last week* senshu
*last month* sen getsu
*at last!* tsui ni
*late: it's getting late* moh osoi desu
*the train is late* densha wa okurete imasu
*laugh* warai
*launderette* koin-randorih
*laundry* (place) kurihningu ya
(dirty clothes) sentaku-mono
*law* (field of study) hohritsu/hohgaku
*lawyer* bengoshi
*laxative* gezai
*lazy: he is lazy* kare wa namake-mono desu
*leaf* ha/happa
*leaflet* chirashi
*learn* narau/manabu
*leather* kawa
*leave* (go away) deru/saru
(object) nokosu
*lecture* kohgi
*lecturer* kohshi
*left* (not right) hidari
*turn left* hidari ni magatte kudasai
*left luggage* tenimotsu azukarisho
(locker) rokkah
*leg* ashi
*leisure* reyjah
*lemon* remon
*lemonade* remonehdo
*length* nagasa

*lens* renzu
*less: less than... ...yori* sukunai
*lesson* jugyoh
*letter* tegami
*letterbox* yu-bimbako
*lettuce* retasu
*library* toshokan
*licence* menkyo
*life* seikatsu
*lift* (in building) erebehtah
*could you give me a lift?* nosete kure-masenka
*light* (not heavy) karui
(not dark) akarui
*lighter* raitah
*lighter fuel* raitah no gasu
*light meter* roshutsukei
*like: I like... ...ga* suki desu
*I don't like it* suki dewa arimasen
*I'd like... ...o onegai* shimasu; ...o kudasai
*lime* (fruit) raimu
*line* (underground, etc.) sen
*lip salve* rippu-kurihmu
*lipstick* kuchi-beni
*liqueur* rikyu-ru
*list* risuto
*literature* (field of study) bungaku
*litre* rittoru
*litter* gomikuzu
*little* (small) chihsai
*just a little* hon no sukoshi
*liver* kanzoh
*living room* ima/ribingu
*lobster* ise-ebi
*lollipop* boh tsuki kyandeh
*long* nagai
*how long does it take?* dono kurai kakari masuka
*lorry* torakku
*lost property* wasure-mono
*lot: a lot* takusan
*not a lot* ohku arimasen
*loud: in a loud voice* ohgoe de
*lounge* raunji
*love* (noun) ai
(verb) ai suru
*lover* koibito
*low* hikui
*luck* un
*good luck!* guddo rakku/ganbatte
*luggage* tenimotsu

# ENGLISH TO JAPANESE 151

*luggage rack* nimotsu-dana
*lunch* chu-shoku

# M

*magazine* zasshi
*mail* (verb) yu-soh suru
  (noun) yu-bin-butsu
*make* tsukuru
*make-up* keshohhin
*man* otoko; danseh; hito
*manager* manehjyah
*map* chizu
  *a map of Tokyo* Tohkyoh no chizu
*March* san gatsu
*margarine* mahgarin
*market* ichiba
*marmalade* mahmarehdo
*married: I'm married* kekkon shite imasu
*martial arts* budoh
*mascara* masukara
*massage* massahji
*mat* (straw) tatami
*match* (light) macchi
  (sport) shiai
*material* (cloth) kiji
*matter: what's the matter?* doh shimashitaka
*mattress* mattoresu
*May* go gatsu
*may be* tabun
*me: it's me* watashi desu
  *it's for me* watashi no desu
  *give it to me* watashi ni kudasai
*meal* shokuji
*meat* niku
*mechanic* kikai gishi
*medicine* (tablets, etc.) kusuri
  (field of study) igaku
*meeting* mihtingu; kaigi
*melon* meron
*memory* (computer) memori
*men* (toilet) dansei yoh to-ee-reh
*menu* menyu
*message* messehji
*midday* shohgo
*middle: in the middle* mannaka ni
*midnight* mayonaka
*milk* gyu-nyu; miruku
*million* hyaku-man
*mine: it's mine* watashi no (mono) desu
*mineral water* mineraru wohtah
*minute* fun
*mirror* kagami
*mistake* machigai
  *I made a mistake* machigai-mashita

*mobile phone* kehtai (denwa)
*modem* modem
*monastery* shu-dohin
Monday getsuyoh
*Monday* getsuyoh bi
*money* okane
*monkey* saru
*month* tsuki/...gatsu
*monument* kinenhi
*moon* tsuki
*moped* tansha
*more* motto
*morning* asa
  *good morning* ohayo gozaimasu
  *in the morning* asa ni
*mosaic* mozaiku
*mosquito* ka
*mother* okahsan
  *my mother* haha
*motorbike* ohtobai
*motorboat* mohtah-bohto
*motorway* kohsoku-dohro
Mount Fuji fujisan
*mountain* yama
  *mountain climbing* tozan
*mouse* (animal) nezumi
  (computer) mausu
*moustache* kuchi hige
*mouth* kuchi
*move* ugoku
  *don't move!* ugokanaide
  (house) hikkosu
*movie* eiga
Mr, Mrs, Ms -san
*much: not much* sukoshi
  *much better* zutto ih desu
*mug* kappu
*mum* okahsan
*museum* hakubutsu kan
*mushroom* kinoko
*music* ongaku
*musical instrument* gakki
*musician* ongakuka
*mussels* mu-rugai
*mustard* karashi
*my: my key(s)* watashi no kagi
*mythology* shinwa

# N

*nail* (metal) kugi
  (finger) tsume
*nail file* nehru-fairu
*nail polish* manikyua
*name* namae
  *my name is...* watashi no namae wa...desu
*nappies* omutsu
  *disposable nappies* kami omutsu
*narrow* semai

*near: near the door* doa no chikaku
  *near London* Rondon no chikaku
*necessary* hitsuyoh
*neck* kubi
*necklace* nekkuresu
*need* (verb) iru
  *I need...* watashi wa...ga irimasu
  *...are needed* ...ga hitsuyoh desu
*needle* hari
*negative* (photo) nega
*neither: neither of them* dochira mo...masen
  *neither...nor...* mo...mo...masen
*nephew* oi
*never* kesshite
*new* atarashih
*news* nyu-su
*newsagent* shinbun ya
*newspaper* shinbun
New Zealand Nyu-jihrando
New Zealander (person) nyu-jihrando jin
*next* tsugi
  *next week* raishu
  *next month* rai getsu
*nice* suteki (na)
*niece* mei
*night* yoru
  *two nights* (stay in hotel) ni haku
*nightclub* naito-kurabu
*nightdress* nemaki
*nine* kyu
*nineteen* jyu-kyu
*ninety* kyu-jyu
*no* (response) ihe
  *I have no money* okane wa arimasen
  *no entry* shin-nyu kinshi
  *no problem* ihdesuyo
*noisy* urusai; yakamashih
*non-smoking* (section) kin-en seki
*noodles* men rui
*north* kita
Northern Ireland Kita Airurando
*nose* hana
*not: not today* kyoh dewa arimasen
  *he is not here* kare wa koko ni imasen
  *not that one* sore dewa arimasen
*notepad* nohto
*notes* (money) shiheh
*nothing* nanimo

*novel* shohsetsu
*November* jyu-ichi
  gatsu
*now* ima
*nowhere* dokonimo
*number* (numeral) su-ji
  (telephone) bangoh
*number plate* nambah-
  purehto
*nurse* kangoshi
*nut* (fruit) kurumi
  (for bolt) natto

# O

*occasionally* tama ni
*o'clock: ...o'clock ...ji*
*October* jyu gatsu
*octopus* tako
*of* ...no
  *the name of the street*
  michi no namae
*off-licence* saka ya
*office* jimusho
  *office worker* kaisha in
*often* yoku/tabi tabi
*oil* oiru; sekiyu
*ointment* nankoh
*OK* okkeh
*old* (thing) furui
  (person) toshi o
  totta
*olive* orihbu
*omelette* omuretsu
*on* ue
  *on the table*
  tehburu no ue ni
*one* (numeral) ichi
  (+ noun) hitotsu (no)
*one way* ippoh tsu-
  koh
*onion* tamanegi
*only* ...dake
*open* (adj) aita
  (verb) akeru
  *what time do you
  open?* nanji ni
  akimasuka
*opening times*
  (museums/libraries)
  kaikan jiman;
  (shops/restaurants)
  eigyoh jikan
*operating theatre*
  shujyutsu shitsu
*opposite: opposite the
  hotel* hoteru no hantai
  gawa
*or* soretomo/aruiwa
*orange* (colour) orenji-
  iro (no)
  (fruit) orenji
*orange juice* orenj
  jyusu
*orchestra* ohkesutora
*order* (noun) chu-mon;
  ohdah
*ordinary* futsu- no
*our* watashi tachi no
  *it's ours* watashi tachi
  no (mono) desu

*out: he's out*
  kare wa gaishutsu
  shite imasu
*outside* soto
*over* (more than) ijyoh
  (above) ue
  *over there* mukoh
*overtake* oikosu
*oyster* kaki

# P

*Pacific Ocean* Taiheiyoh
*package* (parcel)
  kozutsumi
*packet* pakku
  *a packet of...*
  ...hitohako
*pack of cards* kahdo
  hitokumi
*padlock* nankinjoh
*page* pehji
*pain* itai; itami
*paint* (noun) penki
*painting* (hobby) e o
  kaku koto
*pair* futatsu (no)/
  ittsui (no)
  *a pair of shoes* kutsu
  issoku
*Pakistan* Pakistan
*Pakistani*
  (person) pakistan jin
  (adj) pakistan no
*pale* (face) kaoiro ga
  warui
  (colour) usui
*pancakes* pankehki
*paper* kami
  (newspaper) shinbun
*parcel* kozutsumi
*pardon?* e? nan desuka
*parents* ryohshin
*park* (noun) kohen
  (verb) chu-sha suru
*parking: no parking*
  chuusha kinshi
  *parking space* shako
*party* (celebration)
  pahtih
  (group) dantai
  (political) seitoh
*passenger* ryokyaku
*passport* pasupohto
  *passport control*
  (entering) nyu-koku
  shinsa
  (leaving) shukkoku
  shinsa
*path* komichi
*patient* (in hospital)
  byoh-nin
*pavement* hodoh
*pay* harau
  *where can I pay?*
  doko de harae masuka
*payment* shiharai
*peach* momo/pihchi
*peanuts* pihnatsu
*pear* nashi
*pearl* shinju/pahru

*peas* mame
*pedestrian* hokohsha
*peg* (clothes) sentaku-
  basami
*pen* pen
*pencil* enpitsu
*pencil sharpener*
  enpitsu kezuri
*penfriend* penparu
*peninsula* hantoh
*penknife* chihsai naifu
*people* hitobito
  (nation) kokumin
*pepper* (condiment)
  koshoh
  (vegetable) pihman
*peppermints* hakka-
  dorop/minto
*per* ...ni tsuki
  *per person* hitori ni
  tsuki
*perfect* kanzen (na)
*perfume* kohsui
*perhaps* tabun
*perm* pahma
*petrol* gasorin
*petrol station* gassorin
  sutando
*petticoat* pechikohto
*phonecard* tereka;
  terehon cahdo
*photocopier* kopihki
*photocopy* kopih
*photograph* (noun)
  shashin
  (verb) shashin o toru
*photographer*
  shashinka
*phrase book*
  furehzubukku
*physics* (field of study)
  butsuri
*piano* piano
*pickpocket* suri
  *I've been pickpocketed*
  surare mashita
*picnic* pikunikku
*piece* hitokire/hitotsu
*pig* buta
*pillow* makura
*pilot* pairotto
*pin* pin
*pine* (tree) matsu
*pineapple* painappuru
*pink* pinku
*pipe* (for smoking)
  paip
  (for water)
  suidohkan
*pizza* piza
*place* basho
*plants* shokubutsu
*plaster* (for cut)
  bansohkoh
*plastic* purasuchikku
*plastic bag* binihru-
  bukuro
*plate* sara
*platform* purrattohohmu
*play* (theatre) geki/
  shibai

*pleasant* kimochi no ih
*please* (give me)
  (o) onegai shimasu
  (please do) dohzo
*plug* (electrical)
  konsento
  (sink) sen
*plumber* haikankoh
*pocket* poketto
*poison* doku
*police* kehsatsu
*police officer* kehsatsu
  kan; omawarisan
*police report* tsuh-hoh
*police station* kehsatsu
  sho
*politics* seiji
*pond* ike
*poor* mazushih
  (bad quality) shitsu
  ga warui
*pop music* poppu
*pork* butaniku/pohku
*port* (harbour) minato
*porter* pohtah
  (railway station)
  akaboh
*possible* kanoh
*post* (noun) posuto
  (verb) posuto ni ireru
*post box* posuto
*postcard* hagaki
*poster* posutah
*postman* yu-bin haitatsu
  nin
*post office* yu-bin kyoku
*potato* poteto
*poultry* toriniku
*pound* (money)
  pondo
*powder* kona/paudah
*pram* uba-guruma
*prawn* shiba-ebi
  (bigger) ise-ebi
*pregnant: I'm pregnant*
  ninshin shite imasu
*prescription* shohohsen
*pretty* (beautiful) kireh
  (na)
*price* nedan
*priest* (Shintoh)
  kannushi
  (Buddhist) obohsan
  (Christian) bokushi
*printer* purintah
*private* kojin (no)
*problem* mondai
  *what's the problem?*
  doh shimashtaka
*profession: what's your
  profession?*
  goshokugyoh wa
*professor* kyohjyu
*profits* ri-eki
*public* ohyake
*pull* hiku
*puncture* panku
*purple* murasaki
*purse* saifu
*push* osu
*pushchair* uba-guruma

*put* oku
*pyjamas* pajama
  (traditional
  Japanese) yukata

# Q

*quality* shitsu
*quay* hatoba
*question* shitsumon
*queue* (noun) retsu
  (verb) narabu
*quick* hayai
*quiet* shizuka (na)
*quite* (fairly) kanari
  (fully) sukkari

# R

*rabbit* usagi
*radiator* rajiehtah
*radio* rajio
*radish* daikon
*railway* tetsudoh
*rain* ame
*raincoat* reinkohto
*raisins* hoshi-budoh/
  rehzun
*rare* (uncommon)
  mezurashih
  (steak) re-ah
*rat* dobu-nezumi
*raw* nama (no)
*razor blades* kamisori
  no ha
*read* yomu
*reading* dokusho
  *reading lamp* dokusho
  ranpu
*ready* yohi ga deki-
  mashita
  *ready meals* kakoh
  shokuhin
*rear lights* tehru-ranpu
*receipt* reshihto/
  ryohshyu-sho
*reception* uketsuke
*record* (music) rekohdo
  (sporting, etc.) kiroku
*record player* rekohdo-
  purehyah
*red* aka
*refreshments* nomimono
*registered letter*
  kakitome yu-bin
*relatives* (family)
  shinseki
*relax* yukkuri suru
*religion* shu-kyoh
*remember* oboete iru
  *I don't remember*
  oboete imasen
*rent* (verb) kasu
*repairs* shu-ri
*report* (noun) hohkoku
  sho; repohto
*reservation* yoyaku
*rest* (remainder) sono
  hoka
  (relaxation) yasumu
*restaurant* resutoran

*return* (come back)
  kaeru
  (give back) kaesu
*return (ticket)* ohfuku
*rice* (uncooked) kome
  (cooked) gohan
  *rice cooker* sui-hanki
*rich* (person)
  kanemochi (no)
  (food) kotteri shita
*right* (correct) tadashih
  *that's right* sohdesu
  (direction) migi
  *turn right*
  migi ni magatte
  kudasai
*ring* (to call) denwa
  suru
  (wedding, etc.)
  yubiwa
*ripe* jukushita
*river* kawa
*road* dohro; michi
*roasted* rohsuto shita
*rock* (stone) ishi
  (music) rokku
*roll* (bread) rohru-pan
*roof* yane
*room* heya (space)
  basho/supehsu
*rope* tsuna/rohpu
*rose* bara
*round* (circular) marui
  *it's my round*
  watashi no ban desu
*route* (bus, etc.) sen
*rowing boat* bohto
*rubber* (eraser)
  keshigomu
  (material) gomu
*rubbish* (refuse) gomi
  (poor quality)
  garakuta
*ruby* (stone) rubih
*rucksack* ryukku sakku
*rug* (mat) shikimono
  (blanket) mohfu
*ruins* haikyo/iseki
*ruler* (for drawing)
  johgi
*rum* ramu
*run* (person) hashiru
*Russia* Roshia
*Russian* (person)
  roshia jin
  (adj) roshia no

# S

*sad* kanashih
*safe* anzen (na)
*safety pin* anzen-pin
*sailing boat* hansen
*saki* osake
*salad* sarada
*salami* sarami
*sale* (at reduced
  prices) sehru
*sales* (figures) uri age
*salmon* sake
*salt* shio

same: the same dress
  onaji doresu
  *the same people* onaji
  hito
  *same again please*
  onajino o moh hitotsu
  onegai shimasu
sand suna
sandals sandaru
sand dunes sakyu
sandwich sando icchi
sanitary towels seiriyoh
  napkin
satellite TV sateraito
  terebi/ehseh terebi
*Saturday* doyoh bi
sauce sohsu
saucepan nabe
sauna sauna
sausage sohsehji
say yu
  *what did you say?*
  nan to iware
  mashitaka
  *How do you say…in*
  *Japanese?*
  …wa nihongo de nanto
  ihmasuka
scarf sukahfu
school gakkoh
science (field of study)
  kagaku
scissors hasami
Scotland Sukottorando
Scottish sukottorando no
screen (computer,
  etc.) gamen
screen door (ryokan)
  fusuma
screen window
  (ryokan) shoji
screw neji
screwdriver neji-
  mawashi/sukuryu
  doraibah
scroll makimono
sea umi
seafood shifudo
seat seki
seat belt shihto-beruto
second (adj) nibamme
  (no)
  (time) byoh
secretary hisho
see miru
  *I can't see* miemasen
  *I see* (understand)
  soh desuka/
  wakarimashita
self-employed ji-eigyoh
sell uru
seminar zemi/seminah
send okuru
separate betsu (no)
separated (from
  husband, etc.)
  wakareta
*September* kyu gatsu
serious (situation)
  jyu-dai (na)
  (person) majime (na)

serviette napukin
set (in theatre) setto
seven shichi/nana
seventeen jyu-shichi/
  jyu-nana
seventy nana-jyu
several ikutsuka (no)
sew nuu
shampoo shanpu
shave (noun) hige-sori
  (verb) hige o soru
shaving foam hige-
  soriyoh sekken
shawl shohru
*she* kanojo
sheep hitsuji
sheet shihtsu
shell kai/kaigara
sherry sherih
*Shinto* (adj) shintoh no
*Shintoism* shintoh
ship fune
shirt shatsu
shoelaces kutsu-himo
shoe polish kutsu-zumi
shoe shop kutsu ya
shoes kutsu
shop mise
shopkeeper tenshu
shopping kaimono/
  shoppingu
  *to go shopping*
  kaimono ni iku
shopping trolley
  shoppingu kahto
short (object) mijikai
  (person) (se ga)
  hikui
shorts hanzubon/
  shohtsu
shoulder kata
shower (bath) shawah
  (rain) niwaka ame
shower gel shawah jeru
shrimp ebi
shrine jinja
shutter (window)
  amado
  (camera) shattah
siblings go kyohdai
  *my siblings* kyohdai
sick (ill) byohki
  *I feel sick* kimochi ga
  warui desu
side (edge) hashi
  *I'm on her side*
  watashi wa kanojo no
  mikata desu
sidelights saido-raito
sights: the sights of…
  …no kenbutsu
sightseeing kankoh
silk kinu
silver (colour) giniro (no)
  (metal) gin
simple kantan (na)/
  shinpuru (na)
sing utau
single (one) hitotsu
  (unmarried)
  dokushin

single room shinguru
  ru-mu
single (ticket) katamichi
sink (kitchen) nagashi
sister (older) ane
  (younger) imohto
size (clothes) saizu
six roku
sixteen jyu-roku
sixty roku-jyu
skid (verb) suberu
skin cleanser
  kurenjingu-kurihm
skirt sukahto
sky sora
sleep (noun) suimin
  (verb) nemuru
  *to go to sleep* neru
sleeping bag nebukuro
sleeping pill suimin-
  yaku
sleeve sode
slippers surippa
slow osoi
small chihsai
smell (noun) nioi
  (verb) niou
smile (noun) hohoemi
  (verb) hohoemu
smoke (noun) kemuri
  (verb) tabako o su
smoking (section)
  kitsu-en seki
snack sunakku
snow yuki
so: so good totemo ih
  *not so much…*
  sore hodo… dewa
  arimasen
soaking solution (for
  contact lenses)
  kontactoyoh hozoneki
soap sekken
socks kutsushita
soda water sohdasui
sofa sofa
soft yawarakai
soft lenses softo-renzu
soil (earth) tsuchi
somebody dareka
somehow nantoka/
  dohnika
something nanika
sometimes tokidoki
somewhere dokoka
son musuko san
  *my son* musuko
song uta
soon moh sugu
sorry! gomennasai
  *I'm sorry* sumimasen
soup supu
south minami
South Africa Minami
  Afurika
South African
  (person) minami
  afurika jin
  (adj) minami afurika
  no
souvenir omiyage

*spade* (shovel) suki
(cards) supehdo
*spanner* spana
*spares* yobi-hin
*spark plug* tenka-puragu
*speak* hanasu
*do you speak…?*
…o hanashi-masuka
*I don't speak…*
…wa hanashimasen
*speed* supihdo
*spider* kumo
*spoon* supuun
*sport* supohtsu
*sprain* nenza
*spring* (season) haru
(mechanical) bane
*square* (in town)
hiroba
*stadium* stajiamu
*stage* (in theatre)
butai
*staircase* kaidan
*stairs* kaidan
*stamps* kitte
*stapler* hochikisu
*star* hoshi
(film) sutah
*start* shuppatsu/
sutahto
(verb) shuppatsu
suru
*statement* (to police)
hohkoku sho
*station* eki
*statue* dohzoh
*steamed* (food) mushita
*steal* nusumu
*it's been stolen*
nusumare-mashita
*steps* kaidan
*stereo: personal stereo*
uohkman
*sticky tape* serotehpu
*stockings* sutokkingu
*stomach* onaka
*stomachache* fukutsu
*stop* (verb) tomaru
(bus stop) basutei
*stop!* tomare
*storm* arashi
*stove* (kitchen) renji
*straight on* massugu
*strawberry* ichigo/
sutoroberih
*stream* ogawa
*street* michi/dohro
*string* (cord) himo/
kohdo
(guitar, etc.) gen
*student* gakusei
*stupid* baka
*suburbs* kohgai
*sugar* satoh
*suit* (noun) su-tsu
(verb) au/niau
*it suits you* anata ni
niaimasu
*suitcase* su-tsu kehsu
*summer* natsu
*sun* taiyoh

*sunbathe* nikkohyoku
*sunburn* hiyake
*Sunday* nichiyoh bi
*sunglasses* sangurasu
*sunny: it's sunny* hi ga
dete imasu/tenki ga ih
desu
*suntan* hiyake
*suntan lotion* hiyake
rohshon
*supermarket* su-pah
*supplement* (for fares)
tsuika ryohkin
*suppository* zayaku
*surname* myohji
*sweat* (noun) ase
(verb) ase o kaku
*sweatshirt* torehnah
*sweet* (not sour) amai
(candy) kyandih
*swimming* suiei
*swimming costume*
mizuigi
*swimming pool*
suimingu pu-ru
*swimming trunks*
suiei-pantsu
*switch* suicchi
*syringe* chu-sha ki
*syrup* shiroppu

# T

*table* tehburu
*tablet* jyohzai
*Taiwan* Taiwan
*take* noru
*I want to take the
train* densha ni noritai
desu
*can I take it with me?*
motte itte mo ih
desuka
*we'll take it* kore ni
shimasu
*take away* mochi-kaeri
*takeoff* ririku
*talcum powder*
tarukamu-paudah
*talk* (noun) hanashi
(verb) hanasu
*tall* takai
*tampon* tanpon
*tangerine* mikan
*tap* jyaguchi
*tapestry* tapesutorih
*tax: including tax*
zeikomi
*taxi* takushih
*taxi rank* takushih
noriba
*tea* (Western) kohcha
(Japanese) ocha
*teacher* sensei
*teahouse* chamise
*team* chihmu
*tea towel* fukin
*telephone* (noun)
denwa
(verb) denwa suru/
denwa o kakeru

*telephone box* denwa
bokkusu
*telephone call* denwa
*telephone number*
denwa bangoh
*television* terebi
*temperature* ondo
(fever) netsu
*temple* tera
*ten* jyu
*ten thousand* ichi man
*tennis* tenisu
*tent* tento
*terminal* (airport)
tahminaru
*than* yori
*thank* (verb) kansha
suru
*thank you* arigatoh
*thank you very much*
arigatoh gozaimasu
*that: that bus* ano basu
*what's that?*
a-re wa nan desuka
*I think that…*
…to omoimasu
*theatre* gekijyoh
*their: their room(s)*
karera no heya
*it's theirs* karera no
(mono) desu
*them: it's them* karera
desu
*it's for them* karera no
desu
*give it to them*
karera ni agenasai
*theme park* tehma
pahku
*then* sore kara/soshite
*there* (near you) soko
(over there) asoko
*there is/are…* …ga/wa
arimasu/imasu
*there isn't/aren't…*
…ga/wa arimasen/
imasen
*is there…?* …ga/wa
arimasuka/imasuka
*these: these things*
korera no mono/kore
*these are mine*
korera wa watashi no
(mono) desu
*test* (medical) kensa
*they* karera
*thick* atsui
*thief* yatoh
*thin* usui; (person)
yaseta
*thing* (abstact) koto
(concrete) mono
*think* omou/kangaeru
*I think so* soh
omoimasu
*I'll think about it*
kangaete mimasu
*third* sanbamme
*thirsty: I'm thirsty*
nodo ga kawaite
imasu

*thirteen* jyu-san
*thirty* san-jyu
*this: this bus* kono basu
  *what's this?* kore wa
  nan desuka
  *this is Mr…*
  kochira wa…-san
  desu
*those: those things*
  sorera no mono/sore
  *those are his* sorera
  wa kare no (mono)
  desu
*thousand* sen
  *ten thousand* (ichi)
  man
*three* san
*throat* nodo
*throat pastilles* nodo
  gusuri/nodo ame
*through: through*
  *Tokyo*
  Tohkyoh keiyu
*thunderstorm* raiu
*Thursday* mokuyoh bi
*ticket* chiketto
*tie* (noun) nekutai
  (verb) musubu
*tights* sutokkingu;
  taitsu
*time* jikan
  *what's the time?*
  ima nanji desuka
  *to be on time* yotei
  dohri
*timetable* jikoku-hyoh
*tin* (can) kan
*tin opener* kankiri
*tip* (money) chippu
  (end) saki
*tired* tsukareta
  *I feel tired* tsukare-
  mashita
*tissues* tisshu
*to: to England* Igirisu e
  *to the station* eki e
*toast* tohsuto
*tobacco* tabako
*today* kyoh
*toe* ashi no tsumasaki
*tofu shop* tofu ya
*together* issho ni
*toilet* ha
*toilet paper* toiretto
  pehpah
*tomato* tomato
*tomato juice* tomato
  jyusu
*tomorrow* ashita
*tongue* shita
*tonic* tonikku
*tonight* konya
*too* (also) mo
  (excessive) -sugiru
*tooth* ha
*toothache* ha-ita
*toothbrush* haburashi
*toothpaste* hamigaki
*torch* kaichu dentoh
*tour* tsuah
*tourist* ryokoh-sha

*tourist information*
  *centre* kankoh an-naijyo
*towel* taoru
*tower* tawah/toh
*town* machi
*town hall* shiyakusho
*toy* omocha
*track suit* undoh-gi
*tractor* torakutah
*tradition* dentoh
*traffic* kohtsuu
*traffic jam* kohtsuu-
  jyu-tai
*traffic lights* shingoh
*trailer* (for car)
  torehrah
*train* densha
*translate* honyaku suru
*transmission* (for car)
  toransumisshon
*travel agent* ryokoh dairi
  den
*traveller's cheques*
  toraberahzu chekku
*tray* obon/toreh
*travelling* ryokoh
*tree* ki
*trousers* pantsu; zubon
*try* yatte miru/tamesu
*Tuesday* kayoh bi
*tunnel* tonneru
*tweezers* pinsetto
*twelve* jyu-ni
*twenty* ni-jyu
*twin room* tsuin ru-mu
*two* ni
*type* taipu
  *what type of…do you
  have?* donna taipu
  no…desuka
*tyre* taiya

# U

*umbrella* kasa
*uncle* ojisan
*under* shita
*underground* chikatetsu
*underground station*
  chikatetsu no eki
*underwear* shitagi
*university* daigaku
*until…* ma-de
*unusual* mezurashih
*up* ue
  (upwards) ue ma-de
*urgent* kyu (na)/isogi no
  *it's urgent* kinkyu desu
*us: it's us* watashi tachi
  desu
  *it's for us* watashi
  tachi no desu
  *give it to us* watashi
  tachi ni kudasai
*use* (noun) shiyoh
  (verb) tsukau
  *it's no use* yakuni
  tachimasen/tsukae
  masen
*useful* yakuni
  tatsu/benri na

*usual* itsumo no
*usually* itsumo

# V

*vacancy* (room)
  akibeya
*vacuum cleaner* sohjiki
*vacuum flask* mahohbin
*valley* tani
*valve* ben
*vanilla* banira
*vanity box* (ryokan)
  kyodai
*vase* kabin
*veal* koushi no niku
*vegetables* yasai
*vegetarian* bejitarian
*vehicle* kuruma
*very* totemo
  *very much* totemo
*vest* chokki/besuto
*video games* bideo
  gehmu
*video tape* bideo tehpu
*view* keshiki/nagame
*viewfinder* fainda
*villa* bessoh
*village* mura
*vinegar* su
*violin* baiorin
*visa* biza
*visit* (noun) hohmon
  (verb) hohmon suru
*visitor* hohmonsha
  (tourist) ryokoh sha
*vitamin tablet*
  bitaminzai
*vodka* uokkah
*voice* koe
*voicemail* boisu mehru

# W

*wait* matsu
*waiter* uehtah
  *waiter!* sumimasen
*waiting room* machiai
  shitsu
*waitress* uehtoresu
*Wales* Uehruzu
*walk* (noun: stroll)
  sanpo
  (verb) sanpo suru/
  aruku
  *to go for a walk* sanpo
  ni iku
*wall* kabe
*wallet* saifu
*war* sensoh
*ward* byohtoh
*wardrobe* yohfuku-dansu
*warm* atatakai
*was: I was* watashi
  wa…deshita
  *he was* kare
  wa…deshita
  *she was* kanojo
  wa…deshita
  *it was* sore
  wa…deshita

washing machine sentaku ki

washing powder senzai

washing-up liquid shokki yoh senzai

wasp suzume-bachi

watch (wristwatch) udedokei

(verb) miru

water mizu

waterfall taki

wave (noun) nami

(verb) te o furu

we watashi tachi

weather tenki

Web site Web saito

wedding kekkonshiki

Wednesday suiyoh bi

week shu

welcome! yohkoso

well: I don't feel well chohshi ga warui desu

wellingtons nagagutsu

Welsh Uehruzu (no)

were: we were watashi tachi wa...deshita

you were anata wa...deshita (sing. informal) kimi wa...deshita

they were karera wa...deshita

west nishi

the West seiyoh

Westerner seiyoh jin

Western-style yohfuu

wet nureta

what? nani/nandesuka

wheel (of vehicle) sharin

(steering) handoru

wheelchair kurumaisu

when? itsu

where? doko

which? (of two) dochira

(of more than two) dore

whisky uisukih

white shiro

who? dare/donata (formal)

whom: with whom? dare/donata to

why? naze/dohshite

wide hiroi

wife okusan

my wife tsuma

wind kaze

window mado

windscreen furonto garasu

wine wain/ budohshu

wine list wain risuto

wing tsubasa/ hane

wing mirror saido mirah

winter fuyu

with (together with) ...to issho ni

I'll go with you a nata to issho ni ikimasu

(using) ...de

with a pen pen de

with sugar satoh iri

without ...nashi (de)

without sugar satoh nashide

witness (person) shoh nin

woman onna; jyoseh

women (toilet) fujin to- ee-reh

wood mori/zaimoku

wool yohmoh

word kotoba

work (noun) shigoto

(verb) hataraku

it doesn't work ugokimasen

worktop (kitchen) chohridai

worse motto warui

worst saiaku (na)

wrapping paper tsutsumi-gami/ hohsohshi

wrist tekubi

write kaku

writing paper binsen

wrong: it is wrong machigatte imasu

# X, Y

x-ray rentogen

year nen

yellow ki iro

yen yen

yes hai

yesterday kinoh

yet moh

not yet mada

yoghurt yohguruto

you (sing. formal) anata

(sing. informal) kimi

(plural formal) anata-gata

(plural informal) kimitachi

young wakai

your: your shoe(s) (formal) anata no kutsu

(informal) kimi no kutsu

yours: is this yours? (formal) kore wa anata no desuka

(informal) kore, kimi no

youth hostel yu-su hosuteru

# Z

zen zen

zen Buddhism zenshu

zen garden zendera no niwa

zip chakku/zippah

zoo dohbutsuen

# Hiragana/Katakana tables

Japanese is written in three different script systems: **kanji, hiragana,** and **katakana** (see p.14). **Kanji** are Chinese pictograms which need to be learnt individually, but **hiragana** and **katakana** are "syllabaries", with each character representing a separate syllable. The full syllabaries are given here to help you work out the characters in a particular word. With time, you will become more familiar with the most common characters.

## *Hiragana*

| | | | | |
|---|---|---|---|---|
| あ a | か ka | さ sa | た ta | な na |
| い i | き ki | し shi | ち chi | に ni |
| う u | く ku | す su | つ tsu | ぬ nu |
| え e | け ke | せ se | て te | ね ne |
| お o | こ ko | そ so | と to | の no |

| | | | | |
|---|---|---|---|---|
| は ha | ま ma | や ya | ら ra | わ wa |
| ひ hi | み mi | | れ ri | |
| ふ fu | む mu | ゆ yu | る ru | |
| へ he | め me | | れ re | |
| ほ ho | も mo | よ yo | ろ ro | を wo |
| | | | | ん n |

## *Katakana*

| | | | | |
|---|---|---|---|---|
| ア a | カ ka | サ sa | タ ta | ナ na |
| イ i | キ ki | シ shi | チ chi | ニ ni |
| ウ u | ク ku | ス su | ツ tsu | ヌ nu |
| エ e | ケ ke | セ se | テ te | ネ ne |
| オ o | コ ko | ソ so | ト to | ノ no |
| | | | | |
| ハ ha | マ ma | ヤ ya | ラ ra | ワ wa |
| ヒ hi | ミ mi | | リ ri | |
| フ fu | ム mu | ユ yu | ル ru | |
| ヘ he | メ me | | レ re | |
| ホ ho | モ mo | ヨ yo | ロ ro | ヲ wo |
| | | | | ン n |

There are two signs ( ˝ and ˚ ) that are used to add additional sounds to the characters in the syllabaries. For example, the character ヒ hi can become ピ pi, て te can become で de, and ほ ho can become ぽ po.

In addition, a long dash (–) is used to lengthen katakana syllables. For example, the katakana character テ te is lengthened to テー **teh** by adding this dash: テーブル **tehburu** *(table)*, and the character ピ pi is lengthened to ピー **pih**: コピー **kopih** *(photocopy)*.

# Acknowledgments

The publisher would like to thank the following for their help in the preparation of this book: In Japan: Hajime Fukase, Keihin Kyuko Bus Co., Ltd, Takao Abe, Seitoku Kinen Kaigakan, Koei drug, Ichinoyu group, East Japan Railway Company(JR), East Japan Marketing & Communications, Inc., (JR Higashi Nihon Kikaku), Kenichi Miyokawa, Naoki Ogawa, Yumiko Nagahari. In the UK: Capel Manor College, Toyota (GB), Magnet Kitchens Kentish Town, Canary Wharf plc, St. Giles College, Yo! Sushi.

Language content for Dorling Kindersley by G-AND-W PUBLISHING
Managed by **Jane Wightwick**

Picture research: **Hugh Schermuly, Hajime Fukase**

### Picture credits

**Key:**
*t=top; b=bottom; l=left, r=right; c=centre; A=above; B=below*

*p4/5* **DK Images:** *br; p6/7* **Laura Knox:** *cl; p14/15* **DK Images:** *Paul Bricknell cAl;* **Ingram Image Library:** *cbl, cAr; p16/17* **Ingram Image Library:** *ctr; p18/19* **DK Images:** *David Murray tr; p24/25* **Takehisa Yano:** *cbl.* **Ingram Image Library:** *tcr; p28/29* **DK Images:** *John Bulmer tcr; Dave King cr;* **Ingram Image Library:** *bcr; p30/31* **Alamy RF:** *Comstock Images bcl;* **DK Images:** *cl; p34/35* **Takehisa Yano:** *tcr; p36/37* **DK Images:** *cbr; p38/39* **Takehisa Yano:** *bl-r, tcr, cr; p40/41* **Takehisa Yano:** *bl, tcr, cAr, cr, cBr, cbA, bcr bcrA; p42/43* **Takehisa Yano:** *bl-r, c,cr, crB; p44/45* **Courtesy of Toyota (GB):** *c; p46/47* **Toyota (GB):** *ctr;* **Ingram Image Library:** *cAr;* **Takehisa Yano:** *cr, cl, cAl; p48/49* **Takehisa Yano:** *c, bl, cr; p50/51* **Takehisa Yano:** *tcr;* **Alamy:** *Peter Titmuss cr; p52/53* **Getty:** *Stone: Kiriko Shirobayashi cr;* **Alamy RF:** *Image Farm Inc cAr;* **Takehisa Yano:** *bl-r, cr, cBr; p54/55* **Alamy:** *Frank Herholdt bcl; Jackson Smith cBl;* **Alamy RF:** *BananaStock cl; John Foxx c; ThinkStock tcr;* **DK Images:** *Andy Crawford bclA; p56/57* **Takehisa Yano:** *cl, cAl;* **Toyota (GB):** *bl, cBr; p58/59* **Alamy RF:** *Brand X Pictures cBl; Image Source cAAl;* **DK Images:** *John Heseltine cr; p60/61* **Alamy RF:** *Image Source cAr;* **DK Images:** *Steve Gorton cAAr; Pia Tryde cAr; p62/63* **DK Images:** *Russell Sadur cBr, Jo Foord cr;* **Takehisa Yano:** *bl-r, c;* **Alamy RF:** *Goodshoot cAr; p64/65* **Alamy:** *Arcaid bcrA;* **Alamy RF:** *Diana Ninov cAr;* **Ingram Image Library:** *tcr; p66/67* **Alamy:** *Arcaid cll;* **Ingram Image Library:** *bcr;* **Alamy RF:** *Image Source cr;* **Takehisa Yano:** *bl; p68/69* **Takehisa Yano:** *clAl, clAr, cll, clBl, clBr, ctr, cAr cBr, cbr; p72/73* **Alamy RF:** *Image Source cAr; Comstock Images tcr; p74/75* **Alamy RF:** *Doug Norman bl; p76/77* **Takehisa Yano:** *bcl, bcll, bclll, bcAl, bcAll,cbr; p80/81* **Getty:** *Taxi / Rob Melnychuk bc;* **Ingram Image Library:** *cAr;* **Xerox UK Ltd:** *tcr; p82/83* **Alamy:** *wildphotos.com tcr;* **Alamy RF:** *Momentum Creative Group cAl;* **Ingram Image Library:** *cl; p84/85* **Alamy:** *Brand X Pictures cr;* **Alamy RF:** *SuperStock tr;* **Ingram Image Library:** *crB; p86/87* **Getty:** *Taxi / Rob Melnychuk tc; p90/91* **DK Images:** *cl; David Jordan cAr; Stephen Oliver cr;* **Ingram Image Library:** *cBr; p92/93* **Ingram Image Library:** *cl;* **Alamy RF:** *Pixland cr;* **DK Images:** *Guy Ryecart tr; p94/95* **Alamy RF:** *ImageState Royalty Free bcr;* **DK Images:** *tcr; p96/97* **DK Images:** *ctl; p98/99* **Getty Images:** *Daisuke Morita c;* **Alamy:** *Ian Lambot bl; p102/103* **Garden Picture Library:** *Marie O'Hara b;* **DK Images:** *tcr; James Young cAAr; p104/105* **DK Images:** *Bob Langrish cl(6); Jane Burton bl; Geoff Dann cl(2); Max Gibbs cl(4); Frank Greenaway cl(3); Tracy Morgan c(5); p106/107* **Getty Images:** *Daisuke Morita cr; p110/111* **Alamy RF:** *Stockbyte cl; p112/113* **Ingram Image Library:** *bl; p116/117* **Takehisa Yano:** *bcl, bc, bcr; p118/119* **Alamy RF:** *Pixland tcr;* **Corbis:** *Michael S. Yamashita c; p120/121* **Alamy:** *ImageState / Pictor International cl;* **DK Images:** *bcl; p122/123* **DK Images:** *Judith Miller / Sparkle Moore at The Girl Can't Help It cl; p124/125* **DK Images:** *Bob Langrish cl(6); Jane Burton bcl; Geoff Dann cl(2); Max Gibbs cl(4); Frank Greenaway cl(3); Tracy Morgan c(5);* **DK Images:** *Clive Streeter tl;* **Alamy:** *ImageState / Pictor International cl;* **DK Images:** *bcl; p126/127* **Takehisa Yano:** *cl, cll, clll;* **Alamy RF:** *Image Farm Inc bl; p128* **DK Images:** *Clive Streeter tl.*

*All other studio and location images* **Mike Good**